"JC has a beautiful way of c[...]
up the desire to surrender."

- Jaime Barfield, *Palmetto Pointe Church*

"I've had the privilege of knowing JC Worley for many years, and what stands
out most is his authentic walk with God. Deeper21 reflects the life he lives… one
marked by prayer, fasting, and a genuine desire to help others grow closer to Jesus.
This book will inspire you to seek God more deeply and experience His power in
new ways."

- Dr. Marty Baker, *Stevens Creek Church*

"If you're looking for practicality and power, JC's book on fasting is a must read. I
don't know of a more usable resource on fasting than Deeper21. Every church needs
this in their arsenal."

- Matthew Cornett, *Princeton Church*

"Deeper is more than a book; it's a powerful invitation to spiritual breakthrough. As
his friend, I've watched JC lead with integrity and a deep commitment to the Holy
Spirit. His emphasis on these foundational disciplines isn't just theory—it's the fuel
behind the movement he leads."

- Leonce Crump, *Renovation Church*

"With sincerity and conviction, JC emphasizes the vital role of prayer and fasting
in the Christian life. Pastor JC lives what he preaches—his ministry, writings, and
personal example continue to inspire and strengthen the body of Christ."

- Nick Dalton, *The Jefferson Church*

"Prayer and fasting are spiritual disciplines that have shaken the world and shaped
hearts for thousands of years. "Deeper 21" is a powerful guide to these sacred
practices, not only because JC presents the principles of prayer and fasting with

clarity and practicality, but because his teaching is rooted in a life that truly lives them out."

- Jason Daughdrill, Gateway Church

"JC Worley is a practitioner. This book is a synopsis of the way he lives and leads. As you read, I encourage you to practice the principles shared here."

- Bruce Deel, City of Refuge / MOST

"In Deeper21, JC Worley delivers a powerful and practical guide to the life-changing practices of prayer and fasting. With biblical depth and lived experience, he shows how these disciplines open the door to greater intimacy with God and the release of His power in our lives."

- Joe Dobbins, author of Hope After Church Hurt

"This book demystifies fasting, showing how it awakens spiritual hunger, breaks ruts, and draws us closer to Christ. Pastor JC Worley is someone I have learned from for over a decade now. Anytime he is willing to share his wisdom, I listen. I know this book will bless you."

- Noah Herrin, Way Church

"Deeper21 ignites a surefire way to supercharge your prayer life—by fasting. Drawing on a close study of God's Word and years of practice, J.C. Worley reveals the power of fasting to suppress human appetites and draw our hearts closer to the Lord. If you long for a deep-rooted faith nourished by intimacy with God, then Deeper21 is the essential field guide you need."

- Chris Hodges, Highlands College

"Deeper21 is a book you need! I've watched Pastor JC live out what he writes. He's a man who consistently calls people closer to God through prayer and fasting, not just with his words but with his life."

- Mo Huggins, Mountain West Church

"Deeper21 is a guide to encounter more of the things of God. Pastor JC is one of my closest friends, and I've watched him model this life of faith and obedience behind the scenes. This resource will help you go deeper with God and see amazing things unlocked in your own life."

- Jeremy Isaacs, *Generations Church*

"Most books on prayer and fasting make you feel guilty for not being a monk. This book makes you believe you can actually do this."

- Kyle Jackson, *Cape Christian Church*

"There are numerous opinions and multiple resources on how to pray and how to fast. But for these two rituals to work in a believer's life, it must come from the heart. Pastor JC Worley's example of prayer and fasting in his ministry uniquely qualifies him to write about how going 'deeper' with these two scriptural ordinances can strengthen one's spiritual life and effectiveness in whatever ministry you serve."

- Gary Lewis, *General Overseer Church of God*

"JC is not writing on the power of prayer and fasting in theory, JC is writing about the power of prayer and fasting from experience. Deeper21 is more than something he believes, it's who he is."

- Luke Lezon, *Quay Church*

"Deeper21 is practical, convicting, and relevant. Get it and read it! You'll be glad you did!"

- Allan Mathura, Legacy Pastor, *GO Church*

"This book reminded me that prayer still moves mountains and fasting still breaks chains. If you're hungry for more of His presence, this book will shake you, stretch you, and set your heart on fire."

- Markus McFolling, *Founder of Reach1*

"Every follower of Christ needs to practice these essential disciplines. Pastor J.C. provides practical guidance, inspiring stories, and challenges readers to incorporate prayer and fasting into their personal walk with Christ. His book offers valuable insights and will motivate you."

- Kevin McGlamery, North Cleveland Church of God

"Deeper21 is a must for any Christian wanting more of Heaven on earth."

- Terrence Mullings, History Makers Church

"If you are looking for a dusty book of theory, you can stop reading now. However, if your desire is to embark upon an adventure with JC as your proven guide, strap in.

- Joshua Rice, Ph.D., Dean of the School of Ministry, Richmont Graduate University

"I love "Deeper21" because it's not theory—it's lived. Pastor JC doesn't just teach prayer and fasting; he walks it out. This book is a powerful and practical guide for anyone looking to grow their faith. The stories and insights remind us that these practices open the door to God's presence and power in fresh ways. What I appreciate most is that it doesn't just challenge you—it equips and encourages you to take real steps toward a closer walk with Jesus."

- Dino Rizzo, Executive Director of ARC

"J.C. Worley's newest book is a refreshingly unpretentious guide to fasting and prayer. I highly recommend this plain spoken and encouraging book for individuals. It would also be an ideal guide book for a congregational 21 day fast."

- Mark Rutland, Author, Leader, Speaker, Ph.D.

"JC's passion for prayer and fasting has shaped us and challenged us to go deeper in our own walk with Christ. This book carries that same heart and will inspire anyone who reads it to encounter God in a more powerful and personal way."

- Mayo Sowell, Liiv Church Atlanta

"With wisdom and clarity, Pastor JC Worley provides practical and intentional insight that will take you deeper into God's plan and purpose for your life. This resource will not only inspire you but also equip you to walk in greater intimacy and power."

- Tony Stewart, First Assistant General Overseer Church of God

"In Deeper21, JC not only introduces us to spiritual disciplines but also unpacks the 'why' and the 'how,' offering clear, practical steps to strengthen your faith and daily walk with God."

- Matthew Trexler, The River Church

"JC is one of the most disciplined leaders I know, and his proven life gives weight to every word. If you are ready to go deeper in your faith and pursue God with greater passion, this book is a must-read."

- Michael Turner Sr., Turning Point Church

"In this book, you hear a prophetic call to prayer and fasting from the heart of one of today's most prolific shepherds. His words will inspire you to deepen your pursuit of God and give practical guidance on how to enrich and sustain a life of prayer."

- Dr. Mark Williams, Third Assistant General Overseer Church of God

Deeper 21: Experience the Power of Prayer and Fasting in Twenty-One Days

For more information, contact the author at:
contact@deeper21.com

ISBN 978-1-7373242-3-2 (Paperback)

Printed in USA
First Edition

For more resources and information about prayer and fasting, or to contact the author, purchase bulk copies, or inquire about speaking engagements, email contact@deeper21.com

To Kimberly, Laiklan, and London.

CONTENTS

A HUNGER FOR GOD

"He must become greater; I must become less."
- John 3:30

I love to eat, and I bet you do, too. So when it comes to a book on prayer and fasting, it can feel like we're starting at a disadvantage. We live in a culture that celebrates indulgence rather than restraint, and we're constantly surrounded by food. We've been conditioned to believe we're starving without three full meals a day. So when someone mentions the spiritual practice of fasting, your first thought may be, "That sounds impossible." But it's not! It's countercultural, yes. But impossible? No. And in fact, it's one of the most powerful and freeing practices we've been given.

You've probably prayed before; most people have. Fasting is much less common, though, so for a lot of people, it can be intimidating and unfamiliar. But when fasting is paired with prayer, something powerful happens. It unlocks a deeper level of spiritual clarity, a hunger for God, and supernatural power.

Many Christians are frustrated with their spiritual life. They feel like they're in a slump or a rut, lacking power and passion. They want to experience more answered prayers, and they want to feel like God is using their life for a greater purpose. So how can we break out of that spiritual rut? How can we feel closer to God and less attached to this world? How can we go deeper? God gives us a way through prayer and fasting.

This book has 21 chapters, and is meant to be read over the course of 21 days. As you read, please consider participating with some form of praying and fasting, too. My hope is that you will be inspired to make these spiritual disciplines a consistent practice in your life moving forward. We'll talk about both prayer and fasting throughout this book, but I want to focus on fasting first, since it's less familiar.

Preparing to Pursue God

I've fasted on many occasions in various ways, and the best advice I can give anyone who is considering a fast is to simply go for it! Our church begins each calendar year with 21 days of prayer and fasting, and I have experienced and heard of too many miracles during these times to dismiss them as mere coincidence. Something miraculous happens when you fast and pray!

To be clear, I am not promising that you will get whatever you're hoping for by the time your fast ends. We don't fast to manipulate God or to try to get our way. I am, however, promising something even better than getting what you want. When you fast, you will get what God wants for you, and that's always better.

Fasting is hard, though. It's uncomfortable. It goes against our flesh, and it challenges our routines. We know it's something God values—fasting is mentioned more in Scripture than baptism is.[1] And we know that Jesus fasted and prayed constantly. So there is a tension; like many spiritual disciplines, we know we should do it, but we don't. One survey found that about 27% of American Christians participate in some form of fasting. That's only 1 in 4.[2] I wrote this book to change that.

I hope you will spend the next 21 days praying and fasting. If you consult your calendar, you'll find any number of commitments that will convince you to start later, but don't do that. There will never be a convenient time to begin. Make the decision now to start as you read this book. I've never met anyone who regretted it.

First, you'll need to prayerfully decide what kind of fast to do. There are different types of fasts, each with its own purpose and intensity. Understanding the differences can help you approach your decision with wisdom and intention. Let's look at three different kinds of fasts.

Normal Fast

A normal fast, the most common type of biblical fast, involves abstaining from all food while continuing to drink water. It's what most people refer to when they use the word "fasting," and it's what Jesus modeled during His 40 days in the wilderness. Unlike an absolute fast, a normal fast allows for hydration, making it physically sustainable for more extended periods.

The heart behind a normal fast is simple: to express spiritual hunger that is greater than physical hunger. We choose to go without food in order to train our souls to say, "I want God more than I want lunch. I want His will more than I want to satisfy my cravings."

Many believers today use a normal fast for one to three days, or even longer, depending on their spiritual goals. As your body empties, your soul starts to awaken. You feel hunger pangs, but those become reminders to pray. Your body slows down, but your spirit becomes alert. It's in the emptiness that God often fills us with fresh clarity and closeness.

Of course, fasting can feel uncomfortable. That's part of the point. It reveals how often we turn to food for emotional comfort or distraction. But every time you push past the discomfort and lean into God, your appetite for spiritual things increases, and your dependence on physical things decreases.

Absolute Fast

An absolute fast is the most intense and physically demanding type of biblical fast. It involves abstaining from both food and water for a short, set period of time. This kind of fast is rare in Scripture and should be approached with reverence and caution.

Physically, the human body can typically go several weeks without food, but only about three days without water. For this reason, absolute fasts should be very short, usually limited to one to three days, and should never be done without medical consideration and spiritual guidance.

So why would anyone ever attempt an absolute fast? Because there are moments in life that call for radical surrender—crises, decisions, or spiritual battles where partial measures aren't enough. An absolute fast is a way of saying, "God, I need You more than anything, and I need You now!"

The Bible provides powerful examples of absolute fasting in the stories of Moses, Esther, and Paul, all within contexts of urgency and total dependence. An absolute fast is about total consecration. When you deny yourself even water, you're making the boldest declaration a person can make with their body: "I belong entirely to God."

Partial Fast

A partial fast involves limiting or restricting certain foods, meals, or eating times for spiritual purposes. This is the most flexible and accessible form of fasting.

In a partial fast, you're still eating, but you're choosing less so that you can seek more of God. Whether it's cutting out your favorite foods, skipping a meal each day, or avoiding food during daylight hours, the heart of the fast remains the same: to create space for God by laying something down.

The clearest biblical example of a partial fast is found in the story of Daniel, who abstained from "choice" food to better understand the vision God had given him (Daniel 10:2–3).

While the term "Daniel Fast" is not mentioned in the Bible, it is from this tradition that we get the popular form of partial fasting that emphasizes fruits, vegetables, and water, while avoiding sweets, meat, and rich foods. What matters most is not the type of food you're giving up, but the posture of your heart while you're doing it.

I know a partial fast probably seems like the easiest option. I can attest, though, that the cravings can be equally intense, no matter what kind of fast you choose.

Choosing a Fast

While you can read this book without fasting, you'll get the most out of it if you pair the reading with action. So before you read any further, take a few minutes to pray and ask God what kind of fast is right for you.

It can be tempting to want to do something extreme or impressive in an attempt to earn spiritual credit—even in the act of fasting, our pride can creep in. But fasting is not a competition. While it's true that different fasts can lead to different breakthroughs, you shouldn't feel pressure to prove anything—to others or to God.

Whether it's a 21-day Daniel Fast or a commitment to skip lunch and pray during that time each day, what matters most is that you're fasting with purpose and in pursuit of God. You don't need to have it all figured out perfectly. You just need to begin. Because when you pray and fast with the right heart, God always shows up.

Before You Begin

This book has three parts: The Foundations of Fasting, The Power of Prayer, and What Happens When We Seek.

Part 1, The Foundations of Fasting, lays the groundwork for why fasting matters. It explores biblical examples, the spiritual purpose behind it, and how it trains our bodies and hearts to submit to the Spirit. In this section, we'll unpack the connection between fasting and spiritual warfare, the importance of fasting in secret, and how Jesus practiced it. My goal is to give you the knowledge and encouragement you need as you begin your fast.

Part 2, The Power of Prayer, focuses on building a consistent and meaningful prayer life. I'll share stories of mighty prayer warriors throughout history. You'll learn simple and practical ways to pray, how to pray for miracles, the role of intercession, and how to press through when prayer feels dry. Most importantly, you'll discover that prayer isn't about using the right words, but about coming honestly before God, day after day, knowing He listens, cares, and responds.

Part 3, What Happens When We Seek, explores the results of combining fasting and prayer. These chapters explore what Scripture and history reveal when we earnestly seek God: We hear His voice, experience open doors, break strongholds, receive answers, see revival, and deepen our intimacy with Him. This section invites you to believe that seeking God with your whole heart leads to real change, both in you and through you.

At the end of each chapter, you will find a "Deep Dive," a resource to help you get the most out of these 21 days. The Deep Dive is there to help you go further in your practice of prayer and fasting. In Part 1, I'll show you examples of different fasts found in Scripture that you can consider using. These aren't rules to follow, but examples meant to encourage and guide your personal fasting journey. In Part 2, I'll give you one of seven biblical prayers you can pray in your own voice. And in Part 3, you'll read real-life miracle stories from people who have prayed and fasted during seasons of their life when they needed God to move on their behalf. These testimonies are here to stir your faith and remind you that prayer and fasting still make a difference.

My goal is not only to educate you, but also to inspire you, so that you can better understand why prayer and fasting can be such a powerful practice in your life, and then incorporate them into your spiritual journey.

So, whether you're brand new to prayer and fasting or have done it many times before, I pray this book helps you take the next step. And I pray you'll look back on these 21 days as a defining moment in your walk with Jesus.

Prayer:

Father, as I begin this fast, I come with open hands and a hungry heart. I'm not just giving something up—I'm making room for You. Teach me not only to hunger for You, but to talk with You, listen to You, and walk with You daily. I confess how often I run to food, comfort, or distraction instead of running to You. But in this moment, I choose a better way. Shape me through prayer and fasting. Do in me what only You can do. In Jesus' name, Amen.

PART 1

THE FOUNDATIONS OF FASTING

A Brief History of Fasting

The Bible's first mention of fasting as a spiritual discipline is found in the book of Exodus, where Moses fasts for 40 days on Mount Sinai, followed in Leviticus by a command for all of Israel to fast on the Day of Atonement, also known as Yom Kippur. In the Old Testament, fasting was used in times of grief, repentance, and intercession.

When we reach the New Testament, fasting doesn't disappear—it deepens. Jesus fasted for 40 days before beginning His public ministry, and when He taught, it was with the assumption that fasting was a regular part of believers' lives.

After Jesus' resurrection, the early church continued the practice. In Acts 13, for example, Christians fasted and prayed as part of their worship, seeking God's guidance before sending Barnabas and Saul out for missionary work. Fasting accompanied major decisions, especially those involving leadership, calling, or crisis. It was both an act of worship and a request for divine guidance.

In the earliest years of Christianity, fasting was considered a normal and essential part of the Christian life. Epiphanius (c. 315-403 AD), bishop of Salamis, asked, "Who does not know that the fast of the fourth and sixth days of the week are observed by the Christians throughout the world?" Early Christians fasted twice weekly, intentionally choosing Wednesdays and Fridays to differentiate themselves from the Pharisees, who fasted on Tuesdays and Thursdays.[3]

Leaders like Ignatius of Antioch (c. 35-107 AD) emphasized the importance of self-discipline, suffering, and imitation of Christ. Ignatius encouraged believers to live sacrificially and to detach themselves from worldly pleasures as a way of uniting with Christ. A few centuries later, St. Augustine (354-430 AD) would further articulate the value of fasting, teaching that it was not only a discipline of the body, but also a means of humbling the soul, enhancing prayer, and growing in love for God.[4]

As the Church expanded and its structure became more formalized, fasting took on a more organized form within monastic communities. Monks and nuns often adhered to strict fasting rules, avoiding meat, dairy, and other luxuries, and sometimes going long hours or days with little food. The season of Lent—40 days of fasting and reflection leading up to Easter—became an important practice and expression of the Christian faith.

In more recent centuries, fasting has been practiced during times of spiritual renewal. John Wesley, the founder of Methodism, was a huge proponent. He fasted regularly and refused to ordain ministers who would not commit to fasting weekly.[5] Many modern revivals, prayer movements, and mission efforts have been birthed in seasons of fasting and prayer.

Today, Christians around the world continue to fast, with many churches beginning the year with a 21-day emphasis on prayer and fasting. Maybe that's how you found this book.

When you choose to fast, you join a long line of saints. Here is a summary of those we know fasted in the Bible.[6]

Moses fasted for 40 days and nights when receiving the Ten Commandments, and again when he interceded for the Israelites after they created the golden calf. (Exodus 34:27-28; Deuteronomy 9:9; Exodus 32)

Elijah fasted for 40 days and nights after running away from Jezebel. (1 Kings 19:1-8)

David fasted while he was in mourning over Saul and Jonathan, and after his adultery with Bathsheba, while his child was sick. (2 Samuel 1:12; 12:16; Psalm 35:13)

Hannah prayed and fasted because she wanted a child, and God answered her prayer, leading to the birth of Samuel. (1 Samuel 1:7-20)

Jehoshaphat called on all of Judah to fast when facing a military invasion. (2 Chronicles 20:1-3)

Zechariah fasted for the nation of Israel. (Zechariah 7-8)

Esther fasted, and asked Mordecai to recruit others to fast with her, for three days before she asked the king to save her people. (Esther 4:16)

Daniel fasted in response to God's Word, to seek understanding, and later, he fasted for three weeks after receiving a disturbing vision. (Daniel 9:3, 10:3)

Nehemiah fasted and prayed while mourning the broken walls of Jerusalem. (Nehemiah 1:4)

Ezra fasted and proclaimed a fast for the people after learning about their disobedience. (Ezra 8:21)

The king of Nineveh called for a city-wide fast for repentance after Jonah warned that the city would be overthrown. (Jonah 3:5)

Anna, an elderly, widowed prophetess, fasted and prayed day and night in the temple without leaving! (Luke 2:37)

The disciples of John the Baptist fasted often. (Luke 5:33)

Paul fasted for three days after the encounter with Jesus on the way to Damascus that also left him temporarily blinded. (Acts 9:3-9)

Prophets and teachers at the church in Antioch fasted before sending Saul and Barnabas off for missionary work. (Acts 13:2-3)

Cornelius received a vision from God after fasting and praying. (Acts 10:30)

Jesus fasted in the wilderness for 40 days and nights while being tempted by the devil. (Matthew 4:1-2)

CHAPTER ONE

THE PURPOSE OF SPIRITUAL DISCIPLINES

"The spirit is willing, but the flesh is weak."
- **Matthew 26:41**

Before he became a martyr and hero of the faith, Dietrich Bonhoeffer was a young German pastor and theologian searching for what it truly meant to follow Jesus in a world unraveling.

In 1935, as Adolf Hitler began reshaping the church into a tool of the Nazi state, Bonhoeffer took a different path, founding an underground seminary in a small town called Finkenwalde. It was illegal, it was risky, and it was radical, because it defied the regime while also profoundly shaping the souls of those who studied there.

Finkenwalde wasn't a typical seminary. Students rose early to practice the spiritual disciplines. The students soon understood that "they were not there simply to learn new techniques of preaching and instruction but as initiates into a new manner of being a Christian."[7]

To Bonhoeffer, the disciplines weren't optional—they were essential. They were how a believer became strong enough to stand against pressure, temptation, and fear. He knew that resistance didn't begin in public; it began in private, through practices that formed the soul and trained the body to submit to Christ.

He later wrote in *The Cost of Discipleship*, "Only the one who believes is obedient—and only the one who is obedient believes."[8] Belief and obedience couldn't be separated any more than the soul and body could. True discipleship, for Bonhoeffer, demanded both. That's why disciplines like prayer, confession, study, silence, and fasting mattered so much. They weren't religious rituals. They were how you became the kind of person who could endure suffering and remain faithful in the face of evil.

Bonhoeffer lived out what he taught. In 1943, he was arrested by the Nazis for his involvement in a plot to resist Hitler. He spent two years in prison and was executed in 1945, just weeks before the war ended. But his legacy lived on. The man who stood in faith at the end had been formed by years of quiet, consistent, disciplined surrender to Christ.

Faith Beyond Feelings

Prayer and fasting are powerful spiritual disciplines, but they aren't the only ones. Throughout history, Christians have practiced more than a dozen disciplines to grow their spiritual life and become more like Jesus—disciplines like study, service, generosity, fellowship, and more.[9] What separates fasting from the others is that it is a discipline primarily for the body.

Many Christians have been taught that spirituality is only about our souls and minds. We often think of our faith in terms of what we believe, feel, or know, but not as much in terms of what we do physically. As a result, we tend to view the body as either a source of temptation to suppress or a temporary shell to tolerate until we get to heaven.

But the Bible paints a very different picture. It tells us that God created our bodies (Genesis 1:27), Jesus redeemed our bodies through His resurrection (Romans 8:23), and the Holy Spirit dwells in our bodies now (1 Corinthians 6:19–20). That means our bodies are not distractions from our spiritual life—they are a vital part of it. Real, active faith was always meant to involve the mind, the soul, and the body, fully surrendered to God.

Author Tish Harrison Warren asks a powerful question in her book, *Liturgy of the Ordinary*: "What would it mean to believe the gospel, not just in my brain, but also in my body?"[10]

That's where fasting comes in. Every spiritual discipline serves to help some part of you become more like Christ, and fasting* is one of the most tangible ways for us to bring our physical selves into submission to the Spirit. When we fast, we allow our bodies to participate in the spiritual journey. Fasting is quite literally worshiping with your body. It's prayer, but with your stomach.

When fasting is practiced alongside other disciplines, it helps train your whole self—body and soul—to respond more like Jesus in the real situations you face. Intention is not enough; for a Christian, spiritual disciplines help us to become the *kind* of person who is more like Christ.

We see a vivid example of this in the Garden of Gethsemane. On the night before His crucifixion, Jesus took His disciples to pray, knowing the intense challenges they were about to face. He urged them to stay alert, warning them that while their spirit might be eager, their flesh was weak. But instead of praying, they fell asleep. And when

---

* This is also true for other disciplines, like silence and chastity.

soldiers showed up and Jesus was arrested, they panicked and fled.

If the disciples had stayed awake and prayed with Jesus, we can't say for sure what would have happened, but it's reasonable to believe they might have faced the moment with more courage and clarity. Jesus spent time in prayer and responded with a deep sense of peace. The disciples didn't, and responded with fear and chaos.

Take Peter, for instance. He meant well, he was loyal, and he had the best of intentions. He swore he'd never deny Jesus, even after Jesus warned him otherwise. But when the moment of testing came, Peter crumbled under the weight of instinct and fear. His intentions weren't enough—what he needed was a deeper inner character that had been forged over time.

The truth is, spiritual maturity isn't downloaded at the moment of salvation. It's formed little by little, in everyday choices and consistent habits—*disciplines*. Over time, these practices shape us into the kind of people who are more like Jesus, not just in our beliefs, but in our behavior.

To put it simply, there are certain things Christians must do if they want to become more like Jesus.

Faith brings us into a relationship with Christ, but it doesn't automatically transform our character. That requires intentional choices. Real change comes when we develop new rhythms and patterns in our lives.

Denying Comfort

While many spiritual disciplines, including prayer and study, have an obvious powerful effect, the spiritual effect of fasting can be a bit less apparent.

In his book, *The Spirit of the Disciplines*, Dallas Willard argues that one of the greatest misconceptions in Christianity is the idea that our feelings, ideas, beliefs, and intentions are all that really matter. It is this mistake that leaves us with "a headful of vital truths about God and a body unable to fend off sin."[11]

One reason fasting is so crucial to spiritual growth is that it gives us the opportunity to reject comfort through self-denial. Every day, there's a battle between these two forces happening inside us. Our flesh craves what feels good in the moment, but the Spirit yearns for what leads to life and truth. That's why Galatians 5:17 says, "For the flesh desires what is contrary to the Spirit, and the Spirit what is contrary to the flesh." Fasting is a way to practice choosing the Spirit over the flesh.

When we fast, we're saying "no" to food our body craves for a set time. We're not doing it to punish ourselves, but to learn self-control and make more room for God in our lives. It teaches our body that it doesn't always get to be in charge.

This is important because we live in a world that tells us to follow every craving. "If it feels good, do it." That's the message we hear all the time. But Jesus calls us to a different kind of life. He said, "Whoever wants to be my disciple must deny themselves and take up their cross daily and follow me" (Luke 9:23). That's what fasting helps us practice—denying ourselves in order to follow Jesus more closely.

You may notice that when you fast, you become more impatient or frustrated. That's normal. It doesn't mean fasting isn't working—it means it *is*. Your flesh is used to getting what it wants. When you tell it "no," it pushes back. But every time you feel that discomfort and choose to pray instead of complain, you're training your flesh to submit to the Spirit.

The disciplines of Jesus were not just about information; they were about formation. He didn't just teach the truth—He lived it, embodied it, and practiced it. And He invites us to do the same. So when you fast, don't think of it as giving something up. Think of it as gaining something better. You're saying "yes" to spiritual strength, "yes" to deeper intimacy with God, and "yes" to becoming more like Jesus.

Prayer:
Father, I want to be more like Jesus—not just in what I believe, but in how I live. I confess that I've often chosen comfort over surrender, but I want to change that. Teach me to follow You not just in my thoughts and intentions, but in my habits, rhythms, and physical choices. Help me bring my whole self—body and soul—under Your leadership. As I learn to fast, help me deny the cravings of my flesh to make room for more of You. Shape me through prayer, strengthen me through fasting, and remind me that discomfort can be a doorway to deeper intimacy with You. Form me through obedience so I reflect the heart, power, and love of Jesus. In Jesus' name, Amen.

**EVERY SPIRITUAL
DISCIPLINE SERVES TO
HELP SOME PART OF
YOU BECOME MORE
LIKE CHRIST.**

The Elijah Fast

Emphasis
A Normal Fast for restoration and direction, and spiritual recovery.

Duration
40 Days

Scripture
"The food gave him enough strength to travel forty days and forty nights to Mount Horeb, the mountain of God." **(1 Kings 19:8 NLT)**

When to use
When you're discouraged, depleted, or unsure about your calling.

Cautions
It's less about food, and more about time, solitude, and space.

Tips
Unplug digitally. Walk, rest, journal, and pray. This is a slow, sacred journey back to God's whisper.

CHAPTER TWO

MOTIVATIONS MATTER:
WHY WE FAST (AND WHY WE DON'T)

"When you fast, do not look somber as the hypocrites do, for they disfigure their faces to show others they are fasting. Truly I tell you, they have received their reward in full."
- Matthew 6:16

Before Martin Luther became the leader of the Protestant Reformation, he was a young, scared monk desperately trying to earn God's approval. His decision to become a monk wasn't based on his faith, but on his fear. After a near-death experience during a thunderstorm, Luther committed to monastic life, believing it was the only way to escape God's judgment.[12]

Once inside the monastery, Luther was relentlessly disciplined. He fasted rigorously and spent hours in confession, sometimes confessing even the most minor sins—not because He loved God, but because he was desperately trying to be accepted by God. But the harder he tried, the more tormented he became. Despite all his fasting, praying, and spiritual effort, he felt further from God than ever.[13]

Everything changed when Luther encountered a single verse in the book of Romans: "The just shall live by faith." In that moment, the Gospel became clear to him. Righteousness wasn't something earned through discipline, it was received by grace. That revelation not only changed Luther's life; it changed the course of church history.

Luther still fasted, but his motivation changed. He wasn't trying to prove his devotion or win God's favor. He fasted as a way to humble himself and deepen his dependence on grace. His story reminds us that fasting is not about punishing ourselves or earning approval. It's about creating space for God. When practiced with the right motivation, fasting becomes a powerful means of grace—not to earn, but to receive.

Public Recognition

Fasting was not a new phenomenon when Jesus began his ministry, but its purpose had been hijacked by the Pharisees, who fasted to be seen by others. That's why Jesus warned:

"When you fast, do not look somber as the hypocrites do, for they disfigure their faces to show others they are fasting. Truly I tell you, they have received their reward in full. But when you fast, put oil on your head and wash your face, so that it will not be obvious to others that you are fasting, but only to your Father, who is unseen; and your Father, who sees what is done in secret, will reward you." (Matthew 6:16–18)

First, notice that Jesus said, "*when* you fast." He did not say, "*if* you fast." There was an assumption that anyone who was trying to follow Jesus would be fasting. But even more importantly, Jesus gives us one of many wrong reasons to fast: public recognition.

Jesus wasn't saying that you can't tell anyone you're fasting. Many people choose to fast collectively, so that would be impossible. Instead, I think Jesus is getting at what so many of us crave, which is public affirmation.

After you haven't had any food or certain foods for a few days, your sinful nature will want someone to celebrate your accomplishment. Jesus says if you do that, the recognition itself will be your reward. Instead, keep your fast to yourself and let Jesus reward you.

Our flesh loves attention. We want others to see our sacrifice, admire our discipline, or even be inspired by our example. But Jesus reminds us that if the goal is human applause, that applause is the reward, and it's gone in a moment.

I have a friend who committed to a liquid-only fast with a goal of 40 days. But on day 39, he called me and said, "Hey, want to grab wings?" I laughed and said, "But you've only got one more day! You're almost there!" I'll never forget his response. He said, "If I make it to 40 days, I'll end up bragging about myself and the fact that I hit a goal. But this was never supposed to be about me—it's about becoming more like Christ." So we went to lunch. The point is not that you should always cut your fast short, but that my friend knew his heart and his proclivity to find recognition rewarding. It's a temptation we all face.

But public recognition is not the only trap. Let's look at a few more.

To Lose Weight

We live in a culture obsessed with appearance. Body image, health trends, and weight loss plans dominate a lot of our thinking and advertising. It's easy to let those messages creep into our spiritual life, turning fasting into just another tool for self-improvement.

While it's undeniable that weight loss can be a physical benefit of fasting, fasting for the sole purpose of weight loss is not the same as biblical fasting. If your primary motivation is to lose a few pounds, you're doing a diet, not a spiritual discipline. This can be especially tough when fasting aligns with New Year's resolutions. When you fast for spiritual reasons, any physical benefits are just a bonus, not the goal.

Fasting, when practiced biblically, is an invitation to shift our focus away from ourselves and direct our attention to Jesus. When we fast with the goal of weight loss, we're still placing ourselves at the center.

Now, does that mean weight loss is bad? Not at all. Your physical health matters to God. But when fasting becomes merely another strategy to "fix" your body or meet a fitness goal, it loses its spiritual significance.

So if weight loss happens during your fast, great. Thank God for the side benefit. But don't let that become your motivation. Fasting is not a tool for vanity.

But fasting can be misused in more subtle ways, too.

To Twist God's Arm

You can't manipulate God by starving yourself. The purpose of fasting is not to force God to do what you want, but rather to align your will with His. Sometimes God does answer our fasts with healing, clarity, or a breakthrough. But we must be careful not to turn fasting into a spiritual bargaining chip—"If I fast, then God has to come through." That mindset treats God more like a cosmic vending machine than a heavenly Father. It implies that if we just sacrifice enough, we can pressure Him into giving us what we want.

God cannot be bribed or coerced. He sees the heart behind every fast. When our motivation is manipulation, even if it's subtle, it distorts the purpose of the discipline. Fasting is not about control—it's about surrender. It's saying, "God, I need You more than I need this answer. And even if the answer I want doesn't come, You are still enough."

So yes, bring your requests to God while you fast. Ask boldly. Pray persistently. But fast with an open hand. Don't aim to receive something from God, but to become someone who trusts Him, regardless of what He decides.

The Right Reasons

So if motivation matters, then why should we fast? The truth is, there are many different reasons you can choose to fast. The Bible offers examples of people fasting for repentance, guidance, and breakthrough, just to name a few, and these are all valid reasons. But there is one reason above all others that should be the primary motivation: to offer yourself to Jesus.[14]

At its core, fasting is not about what we give up—it's about who we give ourselves to. Romans 12:1 says to "offer your bodies as a living sacrifice, holy and pleasing to God—this is your true and proper worship." That's precisely what fasting is. It's a physical act of surrender.

In a world that constantly tells us to indulge ourselves, fasting invites us to deny ourselves, not to earn God's approval, but to express our love and devotion. Every time you feel hungry, it's a fresh opportunity to whisper, "Jesus, You're more important than my hunger."

Fasting reorders our desires. It places Jesus back at the center of our lives, even if we didn't realize our priorities had shifted. There's nothing like an empty stomach to remind us that only He can fulfill our cravings.

This is why motivation matters so much. If you fast just to check a spiritual box or to impress others, you'll miss the blessing. But if you fast to offer your whole self to Jesus—to seek His heart, His will, and His nearness—then fasting becomes more than a discipline. It becomes worship.

Prayer:

Father, You see beyond my actions and into my heart. Help me to fast with the right motives—not to be seen, not to earn anything, and not to manipulate, but simply to draw closer to You. I want to offer myself to You fully—body, soul, and desires. Purify my intentions and teach me to fast as an act of worship. When I feel hunger, turn my heart to You. When I feel weak, be my strength. I surrender this fast to You, trusting that You are enough. Be glorified in me. In Jesus' name, Amen.

WE DON'T FAST TO GET
SOMETHING FROM GOD–WE
FAST TO GIVE OURSELVES
MORE FULLY TO HIM.

THE EZRA FAST

Emphasis

A Normal Fast for seeking clarity, direction, and divine protection.

Duration

1 Day (Typically)

Scripture

"Then I proclaimed a fast... to humble ourselves before our God, to seek from Him a safe journey..." **(Ezra 8:21 NASB)**

When to Practice

Before making major decisions (moving, job change, leadership steps, or relational crossroads).

Cautions

It can become a checklist. Stay prayerful and intentional.

Tips

Make a decision journal. Name the transition clearly. Ask God specific questions—and give Him space to answer.

CHAPTER THREE

DISCIPLINING THE BODY, FEEDING THE SPIRIT

"But I discipline my body and keep it under control, lest
after preaching to others I myself should be disqualified."
- 1 Corinthians 9:27 (ESV)

When fasting gets difficult—and it will—it's easy to think of it
as cruel or unnecessary. But fasting isn't about punishing your body—
it's about feeding your spirit. In our culture, the body often calls the
shots: if we're tired, we sleep; if we're hungry, we eat; if we're stressed,
we scroll. But Scripture invites us to a different way of life, where the
desires of the flesh no longer dominate our decisions. Fasting is one
way we place the flesh under the leadership of the Spirit and remind
our bodies who's in charge.

Paul uses athletic language in 1 Corinthians 9 to describe this kind
of discipline. He talks about running a race to win a prize and working
to control his body like an athlete in training. In Scripture, the "flesh"
doesn't just mean your physical body—it refers to the part of you that
resists God's rule and wants to live independently from Him. Fasting
helps retrain your whole self—body and soul—to come under Christ's
authority. This is not self-hatred or asceticism; it's purpose-driven

formation. Paul trains his body so that his life will be useful to God and aligned with the Gospel he preaches. That's what fasting does. It helps us train the flesh to submit to the Spirit.

We all have appetites. Food, comfort, approval, and entertainment aren't necessarily sinful, but they become dangerous when we allow them to rule us. Fasting is a voluntary choice to say, "I will not be mastered by my appetites." It's choosing hunger in the stomach to stir a hunger in the soul. It's a declaration that your spirit is in charge, not your cravings.

The goal isn't suffering; the goal is surrender. But in some ways, you do suffer. The first few times you fast, your flesh will fight back. You'll feel irritable, distracted, or even discouraged. That's normal. But over time, your spirit grows stronger. Your appetite for God deepens, and you begin to experience a new kind of freedom—the freedom of not being controlled by your impulses.

This discipline also spills over into other areas of life. When you can say no to food, you can say no to other temptations, too. You build spiritual resilience. Your emotions come under the leadership of the Spirit. You become more alert to sin and more sensitive to the promptings of God.

In Romans 8:13, Paul writes, "For if you live according to the flesh, you will die; but if by the Spirit you put to death the misdeeds of the body, you will live." That's the invitation of fasting: to partner with the Spirit in putting the flesh in its rightful place—under the authority of Christ.

So as you fast, remember: you're not just skipping a meal. You're engaging in a sacred practice that Christians have been doing for thousands of years. You're learning to deny yourself so you can follow Jesus more closely. You're reminding your body who's in charge. And you're creating space for God to do deep work within you.

This is how we become disciples who are not only saved, but shaped, and not only forgiven, but formed into the image of Christ.

Fighting For Freedom

One of the most compelling historical examples of someone who trained his flesh through fasting is St. Anthony the Great, often called the "father of monks," whose practices were a precursor to monasticism.

Born around 251 A.D. in Egypt, Anthony grew up in a wealthy Christian home. But after hearing Jesus' words in Matthew 19—"...go, sell your possessions and give to the poor, and you will have treasure in heaven. Then come, follow me..."—he did exactly that. He sold everything he had, gave the proceeds to the poor, and went into the desert to seek God.

Anthony was intentionally choosing a life that would confront his flesh and shape his spirit. He recognized early on that the real war wasn't out there in the world—it was inside. He wanted his soul to lead and his body to follow. So he trained it.[15]

He began fasting regularly, often eating only bread and water, and sometimes going days without food. He slept on the ground and rejected comfort. He spent hours each day in prayer, in silence, and meditating on Scripture. To the outside world, it may have looked extreme, but Anthony wanted to be free. He knew that unless the flesh was trained, it would dominate. Unless the appetites were restrained, they would rule.

Early Christian writers, including Athanasius, describe how Anthony faced overwhelming spiritual warfare, including visions, fears, and temptations. Yet he endured, not by accident, but because he had trained his body and mind to submit to the Spirit. The longer he remained in the desert, the stronger his soul became. And while he lived in near-total obscurity, people from all over began to seek him out. They were drawn to his peace, wisdom, and authority.[16]

Anthony didn't set out to lead a movement; he set out to master himself. But his personal obedience inspired generations. Monastic communities all over the world trace their roots back to his life and teachings.

Like the athlete Paul described in 1 Corinthians 9, Anthony disciplined his body for something greater than comfort. The desert was his training ground. His hunger became his teacher. And over time, the man he became was stronger than the cravings he denied.

To be clear, you probably do not live alone in the desert. You're not monastic. You might be trying to pray while your kids bang on your bedroom door. You might be stuck in traffic or having car trouble. You might be trying to raise a teenager or care for a sick parent. When you hear about someone's extreme act for God, there is always a temptation to assume that you're not doing enough, or to feel guilty about the quality of your spirituality.

Anthony's life was far different from yours, but the principle remains: When we humble our flesh, our spirit grows strong. When we deny temporary comforts, we gain spiritual clarity. And when we fast, we follow in the footsteps of the saints who knew the secret to spiritual strength.

So don't despise the discomfort—let it shape you. This is what it means to discipline the body and feed the spirit. On the other side of that growl in your stomach is a deeper hunger for God, and only God has the power to satisfy it.

Prayer:

Father, I want to live a life led by Your Spirit, not ruled by my cravings. Help me discipline my body and bring it under Your authority. When I feel weak or weary in fasting, remind me that I'm not being punished—I'm being formed. Teach me to embrace discomfort as the soil where spiritual strength grows. Shape me through surrender. Train me through self-denial. And fill the empty places with more of You. May my fast not be for show, but for transformation. I offer my body, my desires, and my days to You—fully and freely. In Jesus' name, Amen.

🙏

FASTING ISN'T PUNISHMENT—IT'S TRAINING. YOUR BODY ISN'T IN CHARGE; YOUR SPIRIT IS.

The Daniel Fast

Emphasis

A Partial Fast for spiritual clarity, renewal, and deeper intimacy with God.

Duration

21 Days

Scripture

"I did not eat any tasty food, nor did meat or wine enter my mouth... until the entire three weeks were completed." **(Daniel 10:3 NASB)**

When to Practice

When you need direction, when distractions feel overwhelming, or as a sustainable corporate fast.

Cautions

It's easy to treat like a diet. It requires intentional prayer and worship to stay spiritually focused.

Tips

Prepare meals ahead of time. Journal daily. Don't just change what you eat, also change how you listen for God.

CHAPTER FOUR

GOD SEES

"...your Father, who sees what is
done in secret, will reward you."
- Matthew 6:6

John Hyde was a missionary to India in the late 1800s and early 1900s. He wasn't known for grand sermons or popular books. He wasn't famous during his lifetime. In fact, much of what God did through his life happened behind closed doors.

He would often go without food for days at a time, choosing instead to spend hours, and sometimes entire nights, in prayer. Friends who encountered him were often struck by the intensity of his burden. Yet it all happened out of sight. No spotlight. No applause. Just the quiet, relentless pursuit of God. Hyde would lock himself in a small room and pray until he sensed a breakthrough. Sometimes, his friends would find him face down—weakened from fasting, yet radiant with joy from having met with God.[17]

Despite his anonymity, his results were staggering. In the years of his ministry in the region, revival broke out in northern India. Thousands came to Christ, and entire regions were stirred spiritually. But Hyde never sought the spotlight.

His life embodies Jesus' teaching, "when you fast and pray in secret, your Father, who sees what happens in secret, will reward you." Hyde's power wasn't found in his words—it was found in the quiet hours, the hidden places, and the secret hunger for God.

The Hidden Reward

We've already seen Jesus warn against fasting for public recognition in Matthew 6. But there's more to that teaching—He doesn't just give a warning, He offers a promise. Let's look at the scripture again:

> "When you fast, do not look somber as the hypocrites do, for they disfigure their faces to show others they are fasting. Truly I tell you, they have received their reward in full. But when you fast, put oil on your head and wash your face, so that it will not be obvious to others that you are fasting, but only to your Father, who is unseen; and your Father, who sees what is done in secret, will reward you." (Matthew 6:16–18)

Jesus is clear that fasting is not about impressing others or proving our spirituality. It's not for show. It's for God. And when we fast in secret, Jesus promises something remarkable: the Father sees, and He rewards.

In a world driven by visibility, it's easy to tie our worth to what people can see. We want our spiritual lives to be recognized, affirmed, and even admired. But Jesus points us in the opposite direction. He invites us into a quiet place where no one else is watching.

There's something sacred about doing something just for God. It removes the temptation to measure success by external results. Instead, we begin to care more about what God thinks than what others see.

So what's the reward? Sometimes it's a breakthrough. Sometimes it's clarity. Sometimes it's a deeper awareness of God's presence. Sometimes it's an illogical joy. Sometimes the reward is something you can clearly feel, like renewed strength, spiritual insight, or an answered prayer. The greatest reward is God Himself—His nearness, His voice, His presence. But there's always a reward, because God always delivers on His promises.

The Pharisees made fasting a badge of honor. They wore their hunger as proof of their holiness. But Jesus turned that upside down. He told His followers to put oil on their heads and wash their faces— essentially, "Clean yourself up. Don't make a scene. Let your hunger stay between you and God." This is freeing. It means we don't have to manufacture emotion or seek recognition. We can fast quietly and trust that God is working, even if no one else knows.

We often assume that the people who change the world are the ones with microphones, platforms, and crowds. But in God's kingdom, influence doesn't always mean popularity. John Hyde changed history from his knees. His strength wasn't found in human ability, but in spiritual availability.

Over time, Hyde's prayers shifted from general petitions to focused, Spirit-led intercession. He began to ask God for specific things—first, that one person would be saved each day. Then two. Then four. And by the grace of God, that began to happen. Reports of hundreds of conversions flowed in from regions where Hyde had been praying and fasting. He was never the one preaching at the crusades, but he was always behind the scenes, laboring quietly.[18]

His health deteriorated under the strain of long fasts and sleepless nights. His heart was eventually found to have shifted physically in his chest cavity. Doctors believed it was because of the extended hours spent hunched over in prayer. Hyde wasn't reckless with his body; he was just radically surrendered. He once said, "Self must be emptied, and Christ alone enthroned." That was not just a quote—it was how he lived.

The fruits of Hyde's hidden life were undeniable. Entire communities in Punjab, India, were shaken by the Spirit of God. Churches that had been cold or lifeless were stirred with hunger and revival. Pastors were convicted, believers were revived, and the lost came to Christ in waves. Hyde never wrote a best-selling book or led a global organization, but his legacy has inspired generations of missionaries, pastors, and prayer warriors to take the secret place seriously.

But don't miss this: You don't need to spend days locked in a prayer room to be seen by God. Your 10 quiet minutes before the kids wake up, your skipped lunch to seek Him, your whispered prayers in traffic—He sees it all. In a world that chases the visible, God is still drawn to the private.

Jesus said, "Your Father, who sees what is done in secret, will reward you." That's not just encouragement—it's a promise. It's the assurance we carry into every quiet moment of private devotion. When no one else notices, God notices. When no one else applauds, heaven applauds.

So as you fast—whether for a breakthrough, a burden, or simply a deeper walk with Jesus—do it quietly. Do it with joy. Do it in secret. And believe this: The God who sees what you do in secret is already working on your behalf. Because in the kingdom of God, what's hidden is often what's most powerful.

Prayer:

Father, You see what is done in secret, and You reward it with Your presence. Teach me to fast not for recognition, but for relationship. Strip away pride, performance, and pretense, and awaken a deeper hunger for You above all else. Remind me that true power is not found in the spotlight, but in the secret place with You. As I fast, quiet my soul and sharpen my spirit. Let my motives be pure and my heart surrendered. May my unseen sacrifice bring You glory and draw me closer to Your heart. I fast for You alone, Lord. In Jesus' name, Amen.

GOD SEES WHAT'S DONE IN SECRET AND HE REWARDS WHAT GOES UNNOTICED BY OTHERS.

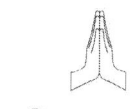

The Corporate Fast

Emphasis

A Normal Fast for discernment, unity, and sending people into ministry.

Duration

21 Days

Scripture

"While they were serving the Lord and fasting, the Holy Spirit said, 'Set Barnabas and Saul apart for Me...'" **(Acts 13:2-3 NASB)**

When to Practice

When launching ministries, appointing leaders, or seeking direction as a family, church or team.

Cautions

Avoid turning it into a performance or checklist. Focus on God's voice, not outcomes.

Tips

Fast together as a group. Begin and end with worship. Record what you sense the Spirit saying collectively and individually.

CHAPTER FIVE

FASTING AND SPIRITUAL WARFARE

"For our struggle is not against flesh and blood, but against the rulers, against the authorities, against the powers of this dark world and against the spiritual forces of evil in the heavenly realms."
- Ephesians 6:12

Before he became the founder of the Jesuits, Ignatius of Loyola was a wounded soldier recovering from a battlefield injury. Bored and bedridden, he asked for adventure novels, but instead was handed books on the life of Christ and the early saints. As he read, something shifted. He began to wonder: What if victory wasn't found on the battlefield, but in surrender to God?

Convicted and drawn into a serious pursuit of Christ, Ignatius did something radical—he gave up comfort, status, and indulgence and retreated to a cave in Manresa, Spain. He lived there in solitude for almost a year, committing himself to fasting, prayer, silence, and repentance.

But it wasn't peaceful. It was war. He was bombarded by spiritual torment—crippling guilt, condemnation, pride, and hopelessness. He even had thoughts of self-harm.

So how did he fight? Ignatius fasted.[19] He humbled his body so he could better hear the voice of God and silence the lies of the enemy.

Through intense discipline, spiritual discernment, and soul-searching prayer, a man trained in military battle became a soldier of the Spirit. He later developed *The Spiritual Exercises*, a training guide designed to help others fight the same inner wars through prayer, fasting, discernment, and surrender.

He discovered what many realize through fasting: When the flesh is silenced, the spirit speaks louder. When cravings are quieted, clarity is found.

Fasting is Fighting

When we think about spiritual warfare, we often imagine dramatic encounters like those of Ignatious—angels fighting demons, intense prayer battles, or moments of high emotion. But there are other examples of spiritual warfare in the Bible that give us another perspective. In the book of Daniel, for example, we see that some of the fiercest battles happen invisibly, behind the scenes, and how fasting plays a significant role in winning them.

In Daniel 10, the prophet is in mourning and prayer for three weeks. He eats no rich food, drinks no wine, and does not anoint himself. It's essentially a partial fast, motivated by a deep spiritual burden. Daniel isn't just seeking answers—he's seeking God. And he's doing so with humility, perseverance, and spiritual hunger.

What happens next is both surprising and deeply encouraging. After 21 days of prayer and fasting, Daniel is visited by an angel. The angel tells him something astonishing:

"...Do not be afraid, Daniel. Since the first day that you set your mind to gain understanding and to humble yourself before your

God, your words were heard, and I have come in response to them. But the prince of the Persian kingdom resisted me twenty-one days. ..." (Daniel 10:12–13)

In other words, the moment Daniel began to pray and fast, heaven heard him. But for 21 days, an unseen spiritual battle raged. The angel who was sent with the answer was delayed by demonic resistance—what the text calls "the prince of Persia"—until another angel, Michael, came to help.

This passage pulls back the curtain on what happens when we fast and pray. There is a spiritual world we cannot see, and fasting strengthens our position in that unseen realm. It releases spiritual power, not because we're strong, but because we're humbling ourselves before the One who is.

When you fast, you're not just giving up food—you're stepping into battle. You're resisting the schemes of the enemy. And sometimes, like Daniel, you may not see an answer right away. That doesn't mean God hasn't heard you. It might mean the battle is still unfolding.

That's why persistence matters. Daniel didn't give up after a few days. He didn't stop when he didn't see immediate results. He stayed faithful and focused, and while he waited, something was happening in the heavens.

This is where many people get discouraged. We assume that if God hasn't answered quickly, then He won't answer at all. But Daniel's story reminds us that delay does not mean denial. Your prayers may already be in motion, stirring things in the spiritual realm, even if you can't see it yet.

Paul reminds us in Ephesians 6:12 that "our struggle is not against flesh and blood, but against the rulers, against the authorities, against the powers of this dark world and against the spiritual forces of evil in the heavenly realms." That means we need spiritual weapons, and fasting is one of them.

Daniel's story reminds us that even if nothing seems to be happening, something is happening. God is always working, sometimes behind the curtain of our understanding, and orchestrating things we'll only recognize in hindsight.

Open Your Eyes

There's another story in 2 Kings 6 when the prophet Elisha and his servant were surrounded by the enemy. The servant was fearful and anxious, but Elisha was calm. He knew something his servant didn't know—God was fighting on their behalf. Elisha prayed for his servant's eyes to be opened, and the servant "looked and saw the hills full of horses and chariots of fire all around Elisha."

Most of us walk through life overwhelmed by what we can see, just like Elisha's servant. We're preoccupied by bills we can't pay, conflicts we can't resolve, habits we can't break, and prayers we've prayed a hundred times. We're panicked by headlines, exhausted by decisions, and worn down by unrelenting stress. It's easy to believe we're outnumbered, outmatched, and on the verge of losing. But just because we can't see it doesn't mean God is not working.

When we fast and pray, we begin to see differently. We remember that we are not alone, that there are more with us than against us (2 Kings 6:16), and that our God still commands angel armies and fights battles we can't see.

Maybe you feel surrounded today by anxiety, doubt, conflict, temptation, or discouragement, like Daniel or like Elisha's servant. But what if you're not as surrounded as you think? What if the armies of heaven are already on the move?

Spiritual warfare is real, but so is spiritual victory. And fasting reminds us that the war has already been won—our role is to stand firm in that truth. When Jesus went to the cross, He didn't just forgive our sins, He disarmed the powers and authorities of darkness (Colossians 2:15). The enemy's weapons still fire, but their power is limited against a believer who is standing in the full armor of God.

Fasting helps us stand. It aligns our will with heaven's agenda. It clears the clutter that often drowns out God's voice. It silences the flesh so we can hear the Spirit. In that stillness, we begin to discern the battle we're in—not just emotionally or physically, but spiritually. And once we know where the battle is, we can begin to fight differently.

Too often, we try to fix spiritual problems with earthly solutions. We distract ourselves with entertainment, bury ourselves in busyness, or numb ourselves with coping mechanisms. But spiritual issues require spiritual solutions. That's why the enemy fights so hard to keep you from fasting—he knows that when you fast, the distractions begin to fall away.

You may not feel strong when you fast. You may feel weak, tired, emotional, or even discouraged. But that's not a sign of failure. In fact, it may be a sign that something is breaking—chains are loosening, walls are cracking, and the enemy knows he's losing his grip.

So fast. Stand. Pray. Like Daniel, you may be closer to your breakthrough than you realize. The battle may be invisible, but the victory is real. The armies of heaven are already advancing.

Prayer:

Father, open my eyes to unseen battles and remind me that You are always fighting for me. When I grow weary, strengthen me. When I feel surrounded, help me see that You surround my enemies. Teach me to trust that my prayers matter, even when I see no immediate answer. Train me to fight—not in the flesh, but through faith, fasting, and surrender. Let my spirit grow strong even when my body feels weak. Thank You for the victory already won through Christ. I choose to stand firm in that truth. In Jesus' name, Amen.

WHEN YOU FAST, YOU DON'T FIGHT ALONE—HEAVEN FIGHTS WITH YOU.

The Esther Fast

Emphasis

An Absolute Fast focused on crisis intervention, supernatural protection, and bold intercession.

Duration

3 Days

Scripture

"Do not eat or drink for three days, night or day... I and my attendants will also fast in the same way." **(Esther 4:16 NASB)**

When to Practice

In urgent moments of spiritual warfare, leadership challenges, or threats to your future.

Cautions

Not safe for everyone. Consult your doctor if needed.

Tips

Gather others to fast with you. Prepare spiritually and physically. Prioritize worship and focused intercession.

CHAPTER SIX

A HUNGER FOR HOLINESS

"Declare a holy fast; call a sacred assembly. Summon
the elders and all who live in the land to the house of
the Lord your God, and cry out to the Lord."
- Joel 1:14

In 1901, missionary Jonathan Goforth returned to China after some time away, feeling a growing dissatisfaction with the results of his work. When he started, he was certain that a harvest would result from his efforts, but now 13 years had passed, and the harvest seemed farther away than ever. Restless and discontented, he began to study scripture more intensively and read books about historical revivals.

Goforth wasn't alone. Missionaries and Chinese believers alike began to sense that something was missing—a lack of spiritual power and purity in the Church. After witnessing the revival that was taking place in Korea in 1907, Goforth returned to China with a renewed burden for prayer and repentance. He began preaching a message not of comfort, but of conviction. He called Christians to confess sin and embrace holiness. The results were staggering.

In meeting after meeting, people were overcome by the presence of the Holy Spirit. Individuals stood in services, wept, and openly confessed sins. The people were so moved, they took it upon themselves to establish days for prayer and fasting.[20]

The revival spread like wildfire. Thousands converted, and the believers who had repented, fasted, and prayed became the spiritual leaders of the house church movement after the communist regime forced the church underground.[21]

Fasting and Repentance

When we choose to fast, we are doing more than giving up food; we are opening up space for God to speak, for the Spirit to search us, and for sin to be revealed. In that space, conviction rises. Things we had ignored, justified, or brushed aside come to the surface, not to shame us, but to set us free.

Throughout Scripture, fasting is often paired with repentance. The people of Israel fasted when they realized they had wandered from God. In the book of Joel, God calls His people to return to Him with fasting, weeping, and mourning (Joel 2:12). Why? Because fasting has a unique way of softening our hearts. When the body is humbled, the soul becomes more sensitive. What once seemed normal starts to feel heavy, and what was once excused now feels exposed. This is the painful gift of fasting: It brings hidden things into the light.

In our busy, comfortable lives, it's easy to lose touch with God's holiness. We go through routines, attend church, and check off our spiritual to-do list, but pride, lust, anger, envy, or compromise may have taken root beneath the surface. Fasting slows us down long enough to see it.

I have an alarm set on my phone for 1:39 p.m. each day to remind me to pray David's prayer from Psalm 139:23–24 as a way of staying spiritually aware: "Search me, God, and know my heart; test me and know my anxious thoughts. See if there is any offensive way in me, and lead me in the way everlasting."

Fasting creates the environment for that kind of searching. It removes distractions and numbs our usual comforts so that God can lovingly deal with what's hidden. This heart-exposing nature of fasting is not new—spiritual leaders through the centuries have recognized it. Richard Foster writes in *Celebration of Discipline*:

"More than any other Discipline, fasting reveals the things that control us. This is a wonderful benefit to the true disciple who longs to be transformed into the image of Jesus Christ. We cover up what is inside us with food and other good things, but in fasting, these things surface. If pride controls us, it will be revealed almost immediately.... Anger, bitterness, jealousy, strife, fear—if they are within us, they will surface during fasting. At first, we will rationalize that our anger is due to our hunger; then we will realize that we are angry because the spirit of anger is within us. We can rejoice in this knowledge because we know that healing is available through the power of Christ.[22]

One of the greatest dangers in Christian life is not failure, but numbness. We can be so desensitized by culture, media, busyness, and even religious routine that we don't notice how far we've wandered. Fasting wakes us up. It tunes our spirit back to the frequency of heaven. It makes space for the Holy Spirit to convict—not to crush, but to cleanse.

This is why throughout history, revival has always been marked by both fasting and repentance. When God begins to stir hearts, people lose their appetite for worldly things. Hunger for holiness becomes stronger than hunger for food. Tears of repentance flow because the people have caught a glimpse of how far they've drifted.

We see this pattern in the New Testament. After encountering Jesus, Paul fasted for three days, blinded and broken, as God prepared him for a new life (Acts 9:9). Fasting was his response to conviction, a provided space for repentance and surrender.

There's something about an empty stomach that awakens a longing in the soul. The ache of hunger reminds us that there is a deeper hunger beneath it—a hunger for God. And as we say no to food, we're saying yes to something greater.

The truth is, many of us have settled. We've tolerated sin. We've numbed our conscience. We've let compromise creep in. But fasting breaks the cycle. Psalm 51:17 says, "My sacrifice, O God, is a broken spirit; a broken and contrite heart you, God, will not despise." Fasting often leads us into that place. It breaks our pride, humbles our hearts, and makes us desperate again. And in that desperation, God meets us.

So don't be afraid of what fasting might expose—welcome it! Because what God brings into the light, He also washes clean. And when we seek Him with fasting and repentance, He always responds. If you feel conviction rising, don't resist it. Let fasting become your invitation to return to God with a whole heart.

Prayer:

Father, I come to You with a humble heart. Search me, cleanse me, and awaken me. In the space that fasting creates, show me what I've hidden or ignored. Let conviction rise—not to shame me, but to set me free. Break my pride and stir in me a hunger for holiness. Forgive my compromise. Help me hear Your voice. Like the people of Joel's day and the saints of revivals past, I return to You with fasting, weeping, and repentance. As I do, meet me with mercy, power, and renewal. I want to be wholly Yours. In Jesus' name, Amen.

FASTING DOESN'T JUST EMPTY YOUR STOMACH; IT OPENS YOUR HEART TO GOD.

The Nineveh Fast

Emphasis

An Absolute Fast for deep repentance, national
or corporate return to God, and revival.

Duration

3 Days

Scripture

"Then the people of Nineveh believed in God;
and they called a fast..." **(Jonah 3:5 NASB)**

When to Practice

When sin needs confronting, in moments of
conviction, or during calls for revival and renewal.

Cautions

Extremely heavy, and should only be practiced with
medical supervision and clear direction from God.

Tips

Repeatedly read Psalm 51 aloud. Build in quiet reflection.
End with hope and assurance of forgiveness.

CHAPTER SEVEN

GOD KNOWS HOW YOU FEEL

"For we do not have a high priest who is unable to empathize with our weaknesses, but we have one who has been tempted in every way, just as we are—yet he did not sin."

- Hebrews 4:15

In the early 1850s, Hudson Taylor boarded a ship to China. He was a young missionary full of passion and conviction, but once he arrived, reality quickly replaced idealism. He was isolated, misunderstood, and far from everything familiar. He didn't speak the language. He was mocked by locals. He hardly had enough to eat, and at times, he didn't have enough money to buy food at all.

It wasn't the physical struggle that hit him hardest; it was the emotional and spiritual weakness. He felt alone, forgotten, and spiritually depleted. But Taylor pressed on with total dependence on Jesus, and in fact, he later reflected that the trials of those early days were all necessary.[23]

During that dark, lonely time, he found comfort in the truth that Jesus knew exactly how he felt. He wasn't alone in his struggle. Christ Himself had walked that road of hunger, rejection, temptation, and suffering.

Later in life, as the founder of the China Inland Mission, Taylor would train hundreds of missionaries to fast, and to endure suffering and persecution. But he always pointed them back to the lessons he learned while empty and broken in his early years.

The Wilderness Way

Fasting can feel lonely. When you're struggling to stay faithful to your fast, it's tempting to believe no one understands what you're going through—the cravings, the spiritual battles, the moments of weakness. No one else sees your struggle, and you might feel spiritually isolated. Fasting forces you to face everything inside of you that still craves comfort, control, or escape. When your stomach growls and your emotions spike, you may wonder if it's even worth it. And in those moments, you may feel very alone.

But here's the truth that changes everything: *God knows exactly how you feel.* You're not just going without food—you are pressing into a Savior who understands what hunger feels like. A God who has walked through loneliness, temptation, and emotional exhaustion.

Jesus fasted—not just symbolically or theoretically—He actually did it. Matthew tells us that Jesus fasted for 40 days in the wilderness. He was tired. He was hungry. He was alone. And in that vulnerable moment, the devil showed up with temptations that made a lot of sense given the circumstances. That's what makes temptation so dangerous—it often disguises itself as something good, reasonable, or even necessary.

First, Satan tried to tempt Jesus with food: "Turn these stones into bread." Of course, after not eating for 40 days, Jesus was hungry. And you'll be hungry during your fast, too. But this temptation speaks to our larger hunger—our desires, our needs, our cravings—especially when we're most vulnerable.

It wasn't just about bread; it was a test of trust. Would Jesus meet His own needs on His own terms, or would He trust the Father to provide in His timing?

We feel this same pull. The longer you fast, the louder your cravings become—not just for food, but for comfort, distraction, or self-gratification. The enemy whispers, "You've done enough. You've earned a break. Just take a little detour; it's not a big deal." But every time you say no to your craving and yes to God, you're building spiritual muscle. You're learning to depend on God's Word more than your appetites.

Fasting teaches us to wait for God, and to believe that His Word is more nourishing than anything we can grab for ourselves in a moment of weakness. It's a declaration: "God, You are enough."

Next, Satan tried to tempt Jesus with validation: "Throw yourself down—God will catch you."

This was a temptation to force God's hand—to prove Himself through spectacle. Satan was essentially saying, "If you're really God's Son, make Him show it. Do something dramatic and make the world notice."

We do this too. In our fasting, we want instant results. We want spiritual fireworks. We want to feel something. Or we want others to see our effort and admire our commitment.

There is a subtle temptation to turn fasting into a performance—to say, "God, I've been faithful, now You show up," or, "Look at what I'm doing for God! Someone, please notice!"

But Jesus didn't need to prove who He was. His identity wasn't up for debate. He didn't need signs, applause, or affirmation to know He was the beloved Son of God. And neither do you.

When you fast, remember that you're not trying to earn love. You're fasting for the God who already loves you. You don't need to prove your devotion with results. You just need to stay faithful. God sees every unseen act of obedience, and His affirmation is all that matters. If we're not careful, we can become legalistic, turning fasting into a scorecard. But that's not the heart of Jesus. Fasting is not a spiritual performance; it's a relational pursuit.

Last, Satan tempted Jesus with power, essentially saying, "Bow down to me and I'll give you all the kingdoms of the world." The devil offered a shortcut—glory without the cross. Power without pain. But Jesus knew the only real path to lasting victory was through surrender. He refused the offer and chose the long, painful, obedient road.

This is one of the most subtle and dangerous temptations we face—not just in fasting, but in life. It's the temptation to take matters into our own hands. To get what we want by cutting corners. To trade long-term faithfulness for short-term gain.

In fasting, this occurs when we seek quick results. We want God to move on our timeline. We want answers, breakthroughs, and blessings, and we want them right now. Jesus refused the offer. He chose obedience—the painful, narrow road. Why? Because He knew who He was and what He came to do.

Fasting puts that same choice in front of us. Will we chase after comfort, or will we lay it all down in obedience to the Father? By fasting, we say no to shortcuts and yes to surrender. We resist the urge to grasp for control and instead submit ourselves to God's will, God's way, and God's timing.

Jesus didn't give in to these temptations, not because it was easy for Him to resist, but because He was anchored in something greater than His cravings. He was grounded in the truth of God's Word and the assurance of His identity. That's our model.

Finding Grace

When your fast gets hard—and it will—remember that Jesus has walked this road before you. He doesn't stand at a distance with His arms crossed. He walks beside you with empathy and strength. He's not disappointed by your struggle; He understands it.

That's what Hebrews 4:15 is all about. "For we do not have a high priest who is unable to empathize with our weaknesses, but we have one who has been tempted in every way, just as we are—yet He did not sin."

Jesus gets it. He gets you. He knows what it's like to feel weak, weary, hungry, and attacked. And He overcame. That means you can run to Him during your fast, even in your lowest moments, and you'll find grace, not judgment.

The next verse is an even greater promise: "Let us then approach God's throne of grace with confidence, so that we may receive mercy and find grace to help us in our time of need" (Hebrews 4:16).

This is what makes Christian fasting so different. We're not fasting to get God's attention. We already have it. We're not trying to earn His approval, either. We have that, too. We fast because we want less of the world and more of Him.

So when your stomach growls, your energy fades, and your emotions run high, remember: *You are not alone*. Jesus has been there. He's felt the weight of hunger, the pull of temptation, and the pain of loneliness. He overcame it all, and now He walks with you as your strength, your guide, and your advocate.

Fasting will stretch you. It will reveal things in you that you didn't know were there. It will challenge your faith, confront your habits, and awaken your spirit. But don't let the difficulty scare you away. Let it press you deeper into Jesus, the One who knows exactly how you feel and offers you grace for every moment of weakness.

Prayer:
Father, thank You for understanding my weakness. You know the hunger, the struggle, and the weight of temptation—and You overcame all of it. When I feel alone, remind me that You've walked this path before me. Strengthen me when I feel tired. Ground me in truth when I'm tempted to give in. Help me remember that I'm not fasting to earn Your love—I already have it. Let this fast draw me closer to You. Shape my heart, align my desires, and give me grace for every step. You are enough, and in You, I have everything I need. In Jesus' name, Amen.

YOU'RE NOT ALONE–JESUS
KNOWS WHAT IT FEELS
LIKE TO FAST.

The Jesus Fast

Emphasis

A Normal Fast for preparation into ministry, overcoming temptation, and aligning identity with mission.

Duration

40 Days

Scripture

"And after He had fasted for forty days and forty nights, He then became hungry." **(Matthew 4:2 NASB)**

When to Practice

Before stepping into a new assignment or spiritual season.

Cautions

It's extremely long. You should only practice with medical supervision and clear direction from God.

Tips

Consider modified versions (1 meal/day or Daniel-style). Anchor each day in Scripture. Build in rest and reflection.

PART 2

THE POWER OF PRAYER

CHAPTER EIGHT

SET A TIME

"Now when Daniel learned that the decree had been published, he went home to his upstairs room where the windows opened toward Jerusalem. Three times a day he got down on his knees and prayed, giving thanks to his God, just as he had done before."
- Daniel 6:10

In 1925, Mother Elizabeth Dabney and her husband began serving at a small mission in Philadelphia. The neighborhood where they ministered was rough, and full of spiritual darkness. Burdened by the condition of the area and longing for a breakthrough, Mother Dabney cried out to God, asking if He would move in power if she committed herself fully to prayer. She sensed the Lord responding, calling her to meet Him the next morning at 7:30 a.m. by the Schuylkill River.

She was so determined not to miss that appointment with God that she stayed awake the entire night, crocheting to keep herself alert.

At dawn, she made her way to the river. As she arrived, she felt the presence of God and knew He had chosen that very place. Right then and there, she made a radical vow: If God would bless her husband's ministry, tear down spiritual walls, and establish a thriving congregation, she would devote herself entirely to prayer. She promised to meet God every morning at 9:00 a.m. sharp, never once being late.

She also committed to spending her whole day in His presence and fasting for 72 hours a week for two years. During those fasts, she would remain in the church overnight, resting on newspapers or the floor if she became tired.

From that moment on, it was as if heaven responded immediately. God's presence fell like rain. Every morning, she greeted the Lord with joy: "Good morning, Jesus." Her knees became raw from the hours spent in prayer, but she didn't waver. Though her body was weary from the fasts, the Holy Spirit became her strength.[24]

It wasn't long before the mission outgrew its space. Her husband asked her to pray for a larger meeting place, and soon, a local businessman, who had been operating his store for 25 years, closed his doors so the mission could rent the building.

Mother Dabney's extraordinary prayer life caught the attention of many. An article detailing her devotion spread across the globe, sparking a worldwide prayer movement. People from around the world wrote to her—she's said to have received more than 3 million letters—asking how to pray like she did.[25]

Her story reminds us that one person, fully surrendered to God, can shift the atmosphere of a city and inspire a generation to seek Him with fervor. But it also reminds us of something incredibly practical— the importance of setting a time to pray.

Sacred Appointments

It may seem like a simple detail, but setting a time to pray can make all the difference in cultivating a powerful prayer life. Just like any other meaningful relationship, your connection with God deepens when you prioritize intentional, scheduled time together. We don't grow close to friends or family without investing time in them, and the same is true for our relationship with God.

Mother Dabney didn't just say she wanted to pray more—she made a vow to meet God daily at a specific time. That daily appointment became a sacred ritual. It wasn't optional; it was the center of her day. It wasn't because she was being legalistic, either. Her discipline was driven by love and reverence. She expected to meet God, and she built her entire schedule around that expectation.

This principle is also evident in Scripture. Daniel, a man known for his unwavering faith, prayed three times a day, even when it became illegal to do so. Jesus often withdrew to lonely places to pray—early in the morning, late at night, and sometimes all night long. These weren't random moments. They were intentional times carved out of a busy life to be alone with the Father.

In our modern world, where schedules are jam-packed and phones buzz constantly, we need this kind of intentionality more than ever. Eugene Peterson, describing how he had to fight to create the margin to nurture his soul in his early pastoring years, found his solution in making an appointment on his calendar. If someone approached him and asked him to commit to a good and worthwhile obligation, but he replied, "I was planning to use that time to pray," they would respond, "Well, I'm sure you can find another time to do that." But if he said, "I already have a commitment on my calendar," no further questions were asked.

The trick, then, is to get to your calendar before anyone else does. Peterson marked out times for prayer, reading, leisure, solitude, and creative work. There were many tasks for him to accomplish in his day, but he said, "...the only way I have found to accomplish them without resentment and anxiety is to first take care of the priorities."[26]

You don't drift into prayer—you plan for it. Without a plan, prayer gets squeezed out by noise, urgency, and distraction. And when you do make a plan, it signals to your heart that prayer is not a last resort, but a first priority.

We know the stories of the first Christians in Acts and the powerful things that happened when they prayed, but what is often missed is *when* they were praying. On the Day of Pentecost, they were gathered together to pray "at the third hour." When Peter and John healed the man by the gate, they were on the way to their "three o'clock prayer service." When Peter saw the vision on his roof, he was praying at "about noon." God honors intentionality. And when we consistently show up to seek Him, He faithfully meets us there.

It's important to point out that while your set time doesn't have to be in the morning, there is something beautiful that happens when you begin your day with God. Instead of being tossed by the chaos and pressure of life, you anchor yourself in His presence. The famous preacher D.L. Moody said in his biography that he felt convicted if he heard blacksmiths hammering before he was praying.[27] I agree with that sentiment. I made a decision a long time ago to rise early and pray. When you do, you invite His wisdom, His peace, and His direction before you face anything else. You're no longer reacting to life—you're living from a place of spiritual grounding.

It doesn't have to be long or dramatic. Even ten minutes of focused prayer can shift the atmosphere of your heart. What matters is that you show up with sincerity and consistency. Don't wait until you "have time." *Make* time. Set your alarm. Put it on your calendar. Guard it like you would a meeting with someone important, because that's exactly what it is.

And when the routine gets hard—and it will—remember that

faithfulness matters more than feelings. Some days the heavens may feel open, and others you may feel distracted or dry. That's okay. Trust that God is doing more in you than you can see.

So find your riverbank, like Mother Dabney. Choose your "9:00 a.m." and meet God there. You might not start a worldwide prayer movement—but then again, you might. Because when one person commits to consistent prayer, all of heaven takes notice. And history has shown that God loves to change the world through someone who simply shows up.

Prayer:
Father, teach me to be faithful in the secret place. Like Daniel and Mother Dabney, help me set a time to meet with You and keep it sacred. I don't want to rush through life without hearing Your voice. Give me the discipline to show up, even when I'm tired or distracted. Stir a hunger in me for prayer that overcomes every excuse. I believe You meet those who seek You, so I will seek You. Let my time with You shape me, ground me, and lead me. Make me a person of prayer. In Jesus' name, Amen.

YOU DON'T DRIFT INTO A LIFE OF PRAYER—YOU SCHEDULE IT.

Fixed-Hour Prayer

In her book, *Spiritual Disciplines Handbook*, Adele Calhoun provides a resource for "Fixed Hour Prayer" (also known as Praying the Divine Office or Praying the Hours)

What is Fixed-Hour Prayer?
Regular and consistent prayers to God throughout the day.

Scripture:
"Seven times a day I praise you." (Psalm 119:164)

Practice Includes:
- Interrupting work at set times for prayer
- Following the prayers in the Liturgy of the Hours
- Following a personal liturgy for prayer at set hours of the day
- Stopping at the top of every hour for prayer

God-Given Fruit:
- Keeping company with Jesus throughout the hours of the day.
- Turning the heart and mind to God at specific hours of the day and night.
- Growing detached from the all absorbing compulsiveness of work.
- Integrating being and doing in your daily life.
- Developing the ability to hear a word from God in the midst of daily activities.
- Joining the timeless prayer rhythms of the church throughout the ages.

CHAPTER NINE

FIND A PLACE

"But when you pray, go into your room, close the
door and pray to your Father, who is unseen…"
- Matthew 6:6

Life was not easy for Susanna Wesley, often referred to as the mother of Methodism. Her health was poor, her marriage to a penniless preacher was deeply dysfunctional, and she lost nine children in infancy and raised 10 more almost single-handedly. Her home was burned down twice, and her husband was imprisoned twice. Despite her challenges, Susanna gave her children six hours of schooling a day, and gave each of them an additional hour every week of undivided attention.

How on earth did she do all this? How did she survive the loss of nine children, along with the heartbreak of a volatile marriage, without becoming broken and bitter? And how did she manage such a frenetic household while also establishing a Sunday school and educating 10 children, two of whom would rise to the heights of international influence? *Prayer.*[28]

Susanna Wesley was a woman of prayer. It was as she waited on the Lord each day that her strength was renewed again and again. But it wasn't easy. There was nowhere at home she could hide to pray, so whenever Susanna wanted time with the Lord, she would pull her apron over her head. This was her prayer room, and her children knew not to disturb her.

While under her apron, she would pour her heart out to God, mourning her tragedies, interceding for her infuriating husband, and praying for each of her children by name.[29]

That small act shaped history. Two of her sons, John and Charles Wesley, would go on to spark a revival that swept across continents. But it started in a kitchen, with an apron and a woman who carved out space to be with God.

Susanna's story is the perfect example of the kind of simple and honest prayer that God desires. And it reminds us that prayer is not as hard as we often make it. If you create a place to meet God, God will meet you there—even if it's under an apron.

Shut the Door

When Jesus instructed his disciples to pray, he gave one very specific instruction related to the setting. He said, "But when you pray, go into your room, close the door and pray…" In today's world, "closing the door" is often less about closing a physical door and more about creating a space free from distractions. With the constant pull of email, group chats, social media, and breaking news, few things are more essential to a thriving prayer life than having a place where you can disconnect from the noise and be fully present with God.

The truth is, place matters. Not because God is limited to certain locations, but because we are. Our minds and hearts are shaped by patterns. That's why Jesus often went to the Mount of Olives (Luke 22:39). It's why Daniel knelt in the same window three times a day, every day (Daniel 6:10), and it's why Moses went to the tent of meeting (Exodus 33:7–11). These were people who had built rhythms of prayer into the architecture of their lives.

Having a place to pray builds muscle memory for your soul. When you return to that sacred space day after day, it becomes a signal to your spirit: Now is the time to meet with God. Over time, your chair, your porch, your parked car, or your corner of the room becomes holy ground. Your body and soul know what to do when you enter that space.

It's easy to get discouraged in prayer because we expect fireworks every time. But often, prayer is quiet, slow, and unseen. And that's why having a certain place helps. A familiar space keeps you rooted. It reminds you that prayer isn't about performance, it's about presence— God's and yours. It's about consistently showing up.

Your place of prayer can become more than just a routine—it can become a refuge. Life doesn't stop being chaotic just because you follow Jesus. In fact, like Susanna Wesley, you may find yourself navigating seasons of grief, stress, pressure, and relational tension. That's why you need a space where you can consistently return to be renewed, so you can re-enter life with peace, wisdom, and strength.

A place to pray becomes a place to process, to lay down burdens, to weep, to rejoice, to confess, and to worship. It becomes a kind of spiritual anchor that keeps you steady when everything else feels like it's drifting. Even when you don't have the words, just sitting in that place can quiet your heart and remind you that God is near. For me, my place is the "prayer chair" in the front room of our house. The seat is beginning to sag, and the hardwood underneath is worn from use. One day, I'll probably have to replace the flooring—thanks to the casters digging in while I've prayed, wept, wrestled, and worshiped in that exact spot.

Susanna didn't wait for her life to calm down before she prayed. The apron over her head may have looked silly, but it was her sanctuary. And it worked. It changed her, it changed her children, and it changed the world.

If we want to build a lasting, vibrant prayer life, we must also make room—literally. For some, that's a specific chair where your Bible always sits. For others, it might be a corner of the bedroom, a walk in the woods, or even a daily commute in the car where you turn off the radio and talk with God.

That's why the enemy of your soul will do everything he can to keep you out of that space. He'll fill your calendar, distract your mind, and tempt you to believe that prayer is ineffective or unnecessary. But if you push through and prioritize that sacred place, it will become your lifeline.

A prayer life grounded in a place leads to a life shaped by peace. You'll begin to carry the stillness of that space with you into your everyday moments. And just like Susanna Wesley in the chaos of her kitchen, you'll discover that when you consistently meet with God, He consistently meets with you. So find your space. Claim it, protect it, and return often.

Prayer:

Father, teach me to shut the door and meet with You. In the middle of life's chaos, help me carve out space to be still, to listen, and to pray. Let my simple place—however small or ordinary—become sacred ground where Your presence meets my weakness. Give me the discipline to return daily and the faith to believe You are near, even when it's quiet. Like Susanna Wesley, help me build a legacy of prayer, not with perfection, but with persistence. Shape my life through these unseen moments, and may they ripple out in power far beyond what I see. In Jesus' name, Amen.

YOU CAN PRAY ANYWHERE,
BUT THE RIGHT PLACE CAN
BECOME A SACRED PLACE
FOR YOUR SOUL.

The Five P's of Prayer

In his book, *Falling for God*, Dr. Gary Moon gives the Five P's of Prayer. This practical, Spirit-Led guide, helps us quiet our hearts and focus our minds on the presence of God. Prayer becomes less about performance and more about relationship.

PLACE
Find a place for prayer that is quiet, comfortable, and free from distractions. Wherever that place is, consecrate it—and ensure there's no chance of being disturbed.

POSITION
Settle into a comfortable position—not "fall asleep" comfortable, but one that quiets your body and helps your mind focus on God.

PACE
This isn't about the speed or length of your prayer—it's about your breathing. Slow your pace. Inhale deeply, expanding your diaphragm; then exhale slowly while counting from one to four.

PERCEPTIONS
In thoughtful prayer, stay present by noticing physical sensations and observing your thoughts without following them. Don't chase emotional experiences—seek depth of awareness and remain centered on God's nearness.

PURPOSE
The goal of prayer is to be with God. It's not just a task on your spiritual checklist. Prayer is a two-way conversation—you speak to God, and God speaks to you.

CHAPTER TEN

PRAYING SIMPLE PRAYERS

"And when you pray, do not keep on babbling like pagans, for they think they will be heard because of their many words. Do not be like them, for your Father knows what you need before you ask him."
- Matthew 6:7–8

When I first became a youth pastor, we had a group of students who were part of our outreach program. They were new to church, and though they weren't professing Christians, they loved coming, and showed up consistently.

We ended our time together every Wednesday night with a closing prayer standing in a circle, hand in hand. One night during our closing prayer, I felt led to warn the group about the spiritual battles we all face. I said something along the lines of, "Sometimes we just need to bind the enemy and curse the devil!"

After I finished, one of the young men new to our group volunteered to close us out in prayer. My heart was so moved. I thought to myself, "Wow, look at this! All the mentoring and discipleship is really starting to pay off." But before I could even finish that thought, he started to pray, and he let loose a string of curse words that left me completely stunned. I stopped him, and he looked at me in all seriousness and said, "You're the one who said we should curse the devil."

If I'm being completely honest, all these years later I think it might still be one of the most powerful prayers I've ever heard.

Praying Without Pretending

When Jesus taught His disciples to pray, there was obviously no foul language involved—but He did want to make sure they didn't overcomplicate it by "babbling on and on." Because, when we speak real, honest words, we say more than polished words ever could.

Many people assume that the louder or longer they pray, the more likely God is to hear them. But Jesus said His Father isn't like that. He's not moved by spiritual showmanship; He's moved by sincerity. That's good news for us. It means you don't need fancy language to pray. You don't need to "sound spiritual." You don't need a script. You just need a heart that's honest and open before God.

Jesus modeled this when He taught the Lord's Prayer. It's simple and direct, with just over 60 words. No fluff, no filler—just a humble, faith-filled conversation with God. Jesus cuts through all the noise. He doesn't call us to pray with perfect words, poetic flair, or long-winded monologues. Instead, He invites us to speak plainly and honestly.

Think about how you speak to someone you love. You don't try to impress them with big words; you just speak from the heart. That's what God wants from you. You can pray things like:

"God, I'm tired today. Give me strength."

"Lord, I don't know what to do. Help me."

"Father, thank You for being with me."

"Jesus, forgive me. I've messed up again."

"Holy Spirit, lead me today."

These are powerful prayers—not because they're eloquent, but because they're honest.

It's also important to remember that simple doesn't have to mean small. Short prayers can move heaven. Think about the desperate father who cried, "I do believe; help me overcome my unbelief!" (Mark 9:24). Or Peter, who, sinking in the water, simply cried, "Lord, save me!" (Matthew 14:30). Or the tax collector who beat his chest and said, "God, have mercy on me, a sinner" (Luke 18:13). God heard every one of them.

Simple prayers are also sustainable. When prayer feels like a performance, we'll avoid it. When we feel pressured, we'll procrastinate. But when it's simple and relational, we'll return to it again and again. That's why Paul encourages us to "pray without ceasing" (1 Thessalonians 5:17, KJV). You don't pray without ceasing by giving a sermon every time—you do it by developing a habit of constant, conversational prayer with God throughout your day.

You can whisper "help" from your car. You can say "thank You" in the checkout line. You can ask, "What now?" during a hard conversation. You can whisper, "Jesus, help me," while folding laundry. These simple moments become sacred when they're directed toward God. These aren't throwaway prayers—they keep you anchored throughout your day.

One of the greatest lies the enemy whispers is that your prayers don't matter unless they sound impressive. But that's exactly what Jesus came to dismantle. He wasn't impressed with religious leaders who prayed on street corners to be seen by others. He warned against empty phrases and long-winded speeches that were more about performance than connection.

Instead, Jesus tells us that our Father already knows what we need. That means the pressure is off. We don't have to explain everything.

We don't have to convince God to care. He's not grading our grammar. We just need to come to Him with humility.

Sometimes you may not even know what to say—but the good news is that the Holy Spirit helps you. Romans 8:26 says, "... We do not know what we ought to pray for, but the Spirit himself intercedes for us through wordless groans." Sometimes, your tears say more than your words. Sometimes, your silence is filled with more meaning than your speech.

To be clear, Jesus wasn't condemning long prayers—He was warning against empty ones. There's nothing wrong with spending extended time in prayer, pouring out your soul before God. But when prayer becomes a performance or a formula, we miss the point. God doesn't respond to the volume or length of our words; He responds to the posture of our hearts.

That's why some of the most powerful prayers in Scripture are short and raw. Job cried, "Though he slay me, yet will I hope in him" (Job 13:15). Hannah simply wept and moved her lips, and God heard her (1 Samuel 1:10–13). Nehemiah, standing before the king, "prayed to the God of heaven" in a single breath before he spoke (Nehemiah 2:4). These weren't polished speeches.

Don't wait for the perfect moment or the perfect words. Just begin. Whisper a line of honesty. Cry out in confession. Offer a sentence of gratitude.

This is especially freeing when you're in a dry season or dealing with doubt. C.S. Lewis reminds us that "what seem our worst prayers may really be, in God's eyes, our best."[30] That's because they are the most honest and sincere.

So the next time you hesitate to pray because you don't know what to say, remember this: You're not trying to impress God. You're just trying to be with Him. And He loves that. That's prayer. And that's more than enough.

Prayer:

Father, thank You that I don't have to impress You to be heard. You know my heart, and You welcome me as I am. Help me to come to You with honesty, not performance—with real words, not rehearsed ones. Teach me to pray simply and sincerely, trusting that You are listening. Let my prayers be more about connection than perfection. When I don't know what to say, remind me that even my silence can be worship. Draw me close each day with a heart that seeks You. Thank You for being near, even in my simplest prayers. In Jesus' name, Amen.

THE MOST POWERFUL PRAYERS ARE THE MOST HONEST ONES.

A.C.T.S. Model Prayer

The A.C.T.S. prayer model offers a Christ-centered framework for drawing near to God through Adoration, Confession, Thanksgiving, and Supplication.

A - Adoration
Praising God for who He is—His character, holiness, power, and love.

"Praise the Lord for being the awesome God that you are."
"God, I honor You as my Creator, my Redeemer, and my Savior."

C - Confession
Confessing your sins to God and asking for forgiveness.

"God, I confess where I've fallen short."
"I ask for Your mercy and cleansing."

T - Thanksgiving
Thanking God for all He has done, is doing, and will do.

"Thank You, God, for the blessings in my life—seen and unseen."
"I'm grateful for Your faithfulness and provision."

S - Supplication
Bringing your personal needs and the needs of others before God.

"Lord, I ask for Your help in this area of my life..."
"Please bring healing, wisdom, provision, and peace."

CHAPTER ELEVEN

PRAYING FOR A MIRACLE

"And my God will meet all your needs according
to the riches of his glory in Christ Jesus."
- Philippians 4:19

George Müller lived in England during the 1800s and experienced a dramatic transformation as a teenager. Before becoming a Christian, he lived a reckless life filled with partying, drinking, and bad decisions, but everything changed when he heard the gospel. His new faith led him to attend missionary school, but his father didn't support his decision and refused to pay for his education. Desperate for help, George dropped to his knees and prayed for God to provide. Amazingly, a professor knocked on his door just an hour later and offered him a tutoring job. That moment launched George into a life of faith, where he would rely on God for everything.

After finishing school, George got a job at a struggling church. The church wanted to pay him, but they didn't have enough money. To raise funds, they rented pews to wealthy families, giving them the best seats while pushing the poor to the back. George saw this as unfair and unwelcoming, so he convinced the church to stop the practice and refused to take a salary. Instead, he trusted God to meet his family's needs. Even though he had no guaranteed income, George and his family always had food, shelter, and everything they needed.

Later, George felt called to help the many orphaned children in his city. He prayed for God's guidance, and soon, someone donated a building for an orphanage, which quickly filled with hundreds of children in need. With so many mouths to feed and very little money, George made it a daily habit to pray for God's provision. Time and time again, God answered in miraculous ways—unexpected donations of food, furniture, clothing, and money arrived just when they were most needed.

One of the most incredible stories of God's provision occurred one morning when the orphanage had completely run out of food. The housemother came to George and told him, "The children are dressed and ready for school, but we have nothing for them to eat." Instead of panicking, George told her to have the 300 children sit at the tables. Then, he bowed his head and thanked God for the meal they were about to receive, even though there was no food.

Moments later, a knock came at the door. It was the town baker. "Mr. Müller," he said, "I couldn't sleep last night. I felt like you might need bread this morning, so I got up early and baked three extra batches for you."

Before George could even respond, another knock came. This time, it was the milkman. His cart had broken down right in front of the orphanage, and the milk would spoil before he could get it repaired. So he donated ten large cans of milk—just enough for the 300 children.[31]

Over the years, George Müller's orphanage cared for more than 10,000 children. When each child was old enough to leave and live on their own, George would pray with them. He would place a Bible in their right hand and a coin in their left, telling them, "If you hold on to what's in your right hand, God will make sure you always have something in your left."

Where Faith Meets Need

We serve a God who performs miracles, and when we hear incredible stories like George Müller's, we often wish we could experience supernatural moments like those. We want to have unshakable faith that God sees us, knows what we need, and will provide for us. The problem is that everyone wants to experience a miracle, but no one wants to be in a position to need one.

The truth is, miracles often begin with need. They're born in the gap between what we can do and what only God can do. And that's exactly where George Müller chose to live—right in that gap. He put himself in positions where if God didn't show up, everything would fall apart. And time after time, God showed up.

That kind of faith can sound intimidating, especially in a world that constantly tells us to make sure we're covered, secure, and in control. But George Müller lived by a different rule.

Many of us long to see God move, but we often don't give Him room to do it. We work hard to avoid risk, need, or discomfort. We rely on our savings, our plans, and our backup plans. There's nothing wrong with wisdom and planning, but sometimes our safety nets become spiritual substitutes.

Sometimes, God allows us to come to the end of our resources so we can rediscover His. And that's not punishment, it's an invitation. It's in the place of desperation that we start to see what God can do.

The Apostle Paul said, "When I am weak, then I am strong" (2 Corinthians 12:10). That's the paradox of faith. In our weakness, God reveals His strength. In our lack, He shows His provision. In our uncertainty, He reminds us that He's always sure.

You don't have to start an orphanage or live without a paycheck. But you can start by depending on God in deeper ways: Give when it doesn't make sense. Step into a calling that feels bigger than your ability. Ask God to provide where you see no way forward.

The Bible is filled with stories of God meeting people right where they were—in their hunger, fear, uncertainty, and weakness. And your story is no different. You don't have to have it all figured out. You just need to bring Him your need and trust Him with the outcome.

So whatever you're facing right now, take it to God. Be honest. Be specific. And then, instead of worrying, start watching. You may find that the breakthrough begins when you stop trying to fix it all yourself and start depending on Jehovah Jireh, the Provider, the One who never fails.

Prayer:
Father, You are my provider, my sustainer, and my source. I confess how often I try to rely on my own strength, but today I choose to trust You more deeply. Teach me to live by faith—not just in what I say, but in how I depend on You. When I face lack, fear, or uncertainty, remind me that You are already working. Help me to release control and rest in Your perfect provision. I want to live in the gap, where miracles happen. Thank You for being faithful—yesterday, today, and forever. I trust You with every need. In Jesus' name, Amen.

GOD HEARS EVERY PRAYER AND
KNOWS EVERY NEED. YOU CAN
TRUST HIM TO PROVIDE.

The Prayer of Jabez

The Prayer of Jabez comes from 1 Chronicles 4:9-10. Tucked into a long list of genealogies. Jabez prays a simple, bold, four-part prayer:

1 Chronicles 4:9-10
Jabez was more honorable than his brothers. His mother had named him Jabez, saying, "I gave birth to him in pain." Jabez cried out to the God of Israel, "Oh, that You would bless me and enlarge my territory! Let Your hand be with me, and keep me from harm so that I will be free from pain." And God granted his request.

1. God, I Pray for Your BLESSING
"Oh, that You would bless me..."
God, bless me abundantly—not for my sake alone, but so I can overflow with generosity and impact every area of my life with Your favor.

2. God, I Pray for INFLUENCE
"...and enlarge my territory..."
God, enlarge my influence to match Your calling—give me bold vision, fresh anointing, and kingdom-impacting opportunities so I can lead others closer to You.

3. God, I Pray for Your PRESENCE
"Let Your hand be with me..."
God, I long for Your presence—surround me, fill me, and lead me by Your Spirit in every moment, every day, and every step I take.

4. God, I Pray for PROTECTION
"...and keep me from harm so that I will be free from pain."
God, cover me and my family with divine protection—guard our hearts, minds, bodies, and futures from every attack, and surround us with Your angels and peace, every day.

CHAPTER TWELVE

INTERCESSION

"Simon, Simon, Satan has asked to sift all of you as wheat. But
I have prayed for you, Simon, that your faith may not fail…"
- Luke 22:31–32

Rees Howells was a humble Welsh coal miner turned missionary who became one of the most remarkable intercessors of the 20th century. After a deep conversion experience, Rees surrendered everything to God. This surrender would become the foundation of his call to intercession. He didn't just pray about problems; he identified with them. He would often fast, isolate himself, and wrestle in prayer until he sensed a breakthrough had come.

Rees believed that true intercession meant entering into the burden of Christ for the world. It wasn't just saying prayers—it was standing in the gap, often with deep spiritual cost.

Perhaps the most famous season of Rees Howells' ministry was during World War II. As the world spiraled into chaos, Rees and his Bible College of Wales became a spiritual outpost of resistance. While others fought on the battlefield, Rees and his team fought on their knees. They would cancel classes and spend hours in prayer, believing they were called to pray through world events.[32]

During the Dunkirk evacuation in 1940, when more than 300,000 Allied troops were trapped on the beaches along the coast of France, Rees and his team interceded day and night. The mission resulted in a "miracle" evacuation under conditions military experts said were impossible. Calm seas, unexpected fog, and an unusual hesitation from the German army all contributed to what historians now call the "Miracle of Dunkirk."

While military records won't credit the evacuation to the intercessory prayer that took place, Rees and many others believed the success was a direct answer to their prayers. He also prayed for the protection of London during the Battle of Britain, and even for the eventual defeat of Nazi ideology. His prayer life was strategic and prophetic. He would often sense spiritual battles before they appeared in the headlines.[33]

The power of Rees Howells' life was not just in the supernatural outcomes, but in his obedience. He was willing to be inconvenienced, misunderstood, and even mocked, because he believed prayer could change history. Today, Rees Howells stands as a model for believers who want to make a difference in the world. His legacy reminds us that one person, fully yielded to God, can partner with heaven to shape nations and generations.

Standing in the Gap

When we pray, our focus is often on our own needs and requests, and that's completely okay. God invites us to bring our needs to Him. In contrast, intercessory prayer allows us an opportunity to shift our focus to the needs of others.

Intercessory prayer is the act of standing in the gap for someone else. It's a bold, selfless kind of prayer that lifts others before the throne of grace, sometimes when they can't, or even won't, pray for themselves. In Luke 22, we see Jesus modeling this kind of prayer for Peter. Knowing that Satan wanted to sift him like wheat, Jesus said, "But I have prayed for you." What a powerful statement. Jesus didn't just hope Peter would make it—He interceded on his behalf.

When we intercede, we align ourselves with God's heart. We ask for His mercy to cover someone else. We contend for their healing, salvation, protection, or breakthrough. And often, we do it without applause or credit. It's hidden work. But make no mistake—it is powerful work, and one of the most Christlike things you can do. It mirrors the ministry of Jesus, who "lives to intercede" for us (Hebrews 7:25). Right now, at this very moment, Jesus is interceding on your behalf. That means He's still praying, still advocating, still standing in the gap. And when we engage in intercessory prayer, we're joining Him in that holy work.

We need more believers who will intercede on behalf of others. For prodigals. For pastors. For marriages. For nations. For the next generation. The world is in desperate need of spiritual warriors— people who will cry out to God not just for themselves, but for the broken, the lost, and the weary.

Consider Abraham interceding for Sodom. He wasn't afraid to plead with God, even multiple times, for the sake of the righteous (Genesis 18:22–33). Or think of Esther, who risked her life to intercede for her people before the king (Esther 7). Her courageous advocacy saved an entire nation.

You don't have to be talented to be an intercessor. You just need a heart that cares. You can intercede for your family, for your church, for your city, for missionaries, for your enemies, for world leaders—the opportunities are endless, because the needs are everywhere.

Jesus showed us this most clearly on the cross. When He said, "Father, forgive them," He was modeling the very heart of intercessory prayer: standing in the place of those who can't stand for themselves, asking God to pour out mercy instead of judgment. And the world needs that kind of prayer now more than ever. It needs intercessors who will stay up late, crying out for the child who's wandered far from God, who will fast and pray for revival in their city, who will pray with faith for healing, reconciliation, provision, and justice, and who will wage war on their knees for the soul of the culture and the heart of the Church.

So, if God puts someone on your heart, take it seriously. Don't ignore that nudge to pray. You might be the only person standing in the gap for them. Your prayer could be the shield that holds back the enemy, the spark that starts a fire, the key that unlocks a door. So, step into the gap. Cry out to God. Be someone's advocate. Become an intercessor. And trust that your prayers are not in vain. God is listening and He still responds to the prayers of His people.

Sometimes, you'll see answers quickly. Other times, you may never see them on this side of eternity. But that doesn't mean your prayers didn't matter. The prayers of the righteous are powerful and effective (James 5:16). They soften hearts, break chains, open doors, and shift atmospheres. These types of prayers create spiritual momentum that moves the hand of God.

So today, ask God: "Who do You want me to pray for?" Then take a few minutes to do it. You might be surprised how much your heart grows in the process—and how powerfully God responds.

Prayer:

Father, teach me to pray like You—selflessly, boldly, and with compassion. Thank You for interceding for me even when I'm unaware. Today, place people on my heart who need prayer. Give me the faith to stand in the gap, the patience to persist, and the love to carry their burdens. Help me see intercession not as a duty, but as a privilege. May I become someone who prays until breakthrough comes, trusting that You hear every cry. Use my prayers to bring hope, healing, and salvation to those in need. In Jesus' name, Amen.

**DON'T IGNORE THE NUDGE
TO PRAY FOR SOMEONE
WHO COMES TO MIND
WHILE YOU'RE PRAYING.**

Jonah's Prayer

From the belly of a fish, Jonah cries out to God in desperation, acknowledging both God's discipline and mercy. His prayer is a model of repentance, surrender, and renewed obedience.

Jonah 2:1-9

1. God, I Cry Out in DESPERATION (v.2)
God, when I am overwhelmed, drowning in the weight of my choices or circumstances, remind me that You hear even my most desperate prayers.

2. God, I Acknowledge Your SOVEREIGNTY (v.3-4)
God, You are in control even in the storms. I trust that nothing touches my life without first passing through Your hand.

3. God, I Turn My Eyes BACK TO YOU (v. 4,7)
Even when I've run from You, You welcome me back. I fix my gaze on You again—restore my faith and realign my heart.

4. God, I Surrender My LIFE (v.9a)
I surrender not just my situation but my future. I will obey what You've asked and walk in what You've called me to.

5. God, I Declare Your SALVATION (v. 9b)
I confess with my mouth that You alone are my Deliverer. I receive Your grace and thank You for rescuing me—even from myself.

CHAPTER THIRTEEN

DID YOU PRAY?

"The Lord is near to all who call on him…"
- Psalm 145:18

When I first started praying, I struggled to stay focused. I tried everything I could to still my thoughts, but the harder I tried, the faster my mind would race. I even came up with a system: I'd take a sheet of paper and fold it in half. On one side, I'd write my prayer list, and on the other, my to-do list—because while I prayed, I'd suddenly remember emails I needed to send, groceries I needed to pick up, or people I needed to call.

Sometimes I'd ramble, grasping for words that sounded "spiritual enough." Other times, I felt embarrassed to bring personal requests to God—especially when they seemed too small or too selfish. And when I finally finished, I'd often walk away wondering, "Did I really pray? If that was real prayer, shouldn't it have felt more… spiritual?"

Is that you? Has prayer ever left you distracted, unsure, or even a little discouraged? If so, you're not alone. And the good news is that your prayer life doesn't have to be stuck there.

Just Show Up

That nagging question—*Did I really pray?*—reveals something deeper about our assumptions. We often equate the effectiveness of a prayer with how emotional or moving it felt. If we cried, got goosebumps, or sensed an internal shift, we assume we truly connected with God. But if our prayers felt flat, awkward, or dry, we assume they didn't count for much. But that's not how prayer works at all.

Dallas Willard once said that prayer is "simply talking to God about what we are doing together."[34] That definition is freeing. It removes the pressure to perform, and shifts the focus from crafting the perfect sentence to simply engaging in conversation. Prayer, at its core, is about relationship, not ritual. It's about presence, not polish.

Eugene Peterson wrote that "our prayers, whether clumsy or skilled, heretical or orthodox, verbatim from the Psalter or ad libbed from a sinking ship, get us no merit with God. ... God hears anything we whisper or shout, say or sing."[35] In other words, God isn't grading your prayers. He's listening to your heart.

These words challenge the unspoken scorecards we use to measure prayer. Did I feel something? Did I pray long enough? Was I eloquent? Did I say it right? We may never say it out loud, but deep down, many of us believe that real prayer is dramatic and emotional—and if it isn't, we must not be doing it right.

But Scripture and experience tell a different story. Prayer isn't always dramatic—in fact, most of the time, it's not. Most prayer is quiet and unremarkable. It's like meeting with a dear friend for coffee each morning. Not every conversation is earth-shattering, but the consistent presence builds a relationship. Over time, you grow in closeness. You learn to listen. You grow to trust. And you start to change. That's how prayer works, too.

In time, your words and your desires will begin to align with God's. Your heart follows your habits. And your spiritual muscles are formed by showing up even when you don't feel anything at all.

But here's something we don't talk about enough: Prayer is spiritual, yes, but it's also physical.

As we discussed in Chapter 2, your body plays a significant role in your spiritual life. Have you ever noticed how tired you feel when you try to pray late at night? Or how distracted you get when you haven't eaten, or when your mind is racing with stress? What feels like "bad prayer" might just be your physical state getting in the way.

C.S. Lewis saw this clearly. In his satirical classic, *The Screwtape Letters*, a senior demon instructs a junior demon to keep people discouraged during prayer: "Teach them to estimate the value of each prayer by their success in producing the desired feeling; and never let them suspect how much success or failure of that kind depends on whether they are well or ill, fresh or tired, at the moment."[36]

That's precisely what many of us do. We aim for a spiritual feeling, and when the feeling doesn't come, we assume the prayer failed. But that's a lie. Feelings are not faith. And silence is not absence.

The enemy wants you to doubt your prayer life because of how it feels. But God doesn't measure your prayers by your emotions. He honors your presence. He honors your faith. He honors your willingness to keep showing up. So what does that mean for you?

It means you go into a room, close the door, kneel down, and talk to God. You don't need the right mood. You don't need eloquent words. You don't need to feel spiritual. You just need to be there. Sometimes your prayers will feel like fire. Other times, they'll feel like fog. Either way, God is listening. He is present. He is near.

So stop asking, "Was it powerful? Did it work? Did I do it right?"

Instead, ask a much simpler question: "Did I talk to God today?" Because if you did, that's prayer.

It may not always feel life-changing in the moment. But over time, it is. It softens your heart. It forms your soul. It creates a space for God to speak, even if He whispers. And it builds a relationship far deeper than emotional highs could ever go.

So whether you whispered, "Help," or poured out your heart for an hour, if you showed up and talked to God, you did the most important thing of all. You prayed. And that's more than enough.

Prayer:
Father, thank You for always being near, even when I don't feel it. Thank You that I don't need perfect words or deep emotions for You to listen. Help me release the pressure to perform and simply show up. Remind me that prayer is a relationship, not a ritual. Teach me to come honestly, consistently, and without shame. Let my heart grow soft and my spirit grow strong in the quiet, ordinary moments with You. Even when my prayer feels dry, help me trust that You are working. Thank You for hearing me. I'm here. I'm listening. I want to know You more. In Jesus' name, Amen.

**PRAYER DOESN'T ALWAYS
FEEL POWERFUL, AND THAT'S
OKAY. PRAY ANYWAY!**

The Lord's Prayer

The Lord's Prayer (Matthew 6:9-13) is Jesus' model for how His disciples should pray. It's not just words to recite—it's a pattern to follow.

1. Connect With God ("Our Father in heaven...")
God loves when we come to Him as children—loving Him and wanting to be with Him. Call Him Father, and thank Him that you are His child.

2. Worship His Name ("Hallowed be your name...")
Speak God's names aloud—there's power in His name. As you worship Him, you remind yourself of how awesome He truly is.

3. Pray For His Will ("Your kingdom come. Your will be done...")
God's will is perfect, and when we pray His agenda first, we honor His wisdom and trust His sovereignty.

4. Trust Him For Everything ("Give us this day our daily bread...")
God promises to supply all our needs, and He wants us to depend on Him to provide.

5. Give and Receive Forgiveness ("Forgive us our debts...")
Ask God to search your heart, forgive your sins, and help you forgive others—even in advance.

6. Engage In Spiritual Warfare ("Deliever us from the evil one...")
Ask God to expose any lies you're believing and reveal areas of spiritual warfare. Resist the enemy through prayer, speak the name of Jesus, and stand on God's truth

7. Declare His Power ("Yours is the power and glory forever...")
End your prayer by declaring God's power and authority. Remind yourself: His Kingdom rules, His power sustains, and His glory will prevail. Nothing is too hard for God!

CHAPTER FOURTEEN

YES, NO, OR NOT YET

"'For my thoughts are not your thoughts, neither are
your ways my ways,' declares the Lord. 'As the heavens are
higher than the earth, so are my ways higher than your
ways and my thoughts than your thoughts.'"
- Isaiah 55:8–9

Not long after Dallas Theological Seminary opened its doors, the school faced a severe financial crisis that nearly led to its closure. Just before the 1929 graduation, the faculty gathered in President Lewis Sperry Chafer's office to cry out to God for provision. They formed a circle and began to pray. When it was Dr. Harry Ironside's turn, he referenced Psalm 50:10 with bold faith, and prayed, "Lord, You own the cattle on a thousand hills. Could You sell some and send the funds we need?"

While God doesn't always answer right away, this time the response was immediate. As the faculty continued in prayer, a secretary knocked on the office door with urgent news. She handed Dr. Chafer a check for $10,000—exactly the amount needed to keep the seminary open. Some say the generous gift came from a Texas rancher who had just sold livestock. Whoever it was, the timing was unmistakable. God had answered their prayer.

Dr. Chafer turned to Ironside with a smile and said words that would go down in seminary history: "Harry, God sold the cattle!"[37]

Three Ways God Answers Prayer

We love stories like the one from Dallas Theological Seminary, when God's answer comes swiftly and dramatically. In those moments, our faith feels strong, our hearts feel full, and our prayers feel effective. But if you've walked with God long enough, you know those kinds of answers, while encouraging, are not the only way He responds.

God always answers prayer, but not always in the way or on the timeline we expect. In fact, most often, His response falls into one of three categories: yes, no, or not yet.

Sometimes when you pray, God says, "Yes." That's what happened for the seminary faculty. Their need was great, their prayer was sincere, and God met them with a miraculous "yes." The check arrived at just the right time, confirming that God hears and cares. These answers build our faith and often become the testimonies we tell others.

But if we always expect a "yes," we'll be disappointed when God leads us down a different path, because sometimes God says, "No." This is the answer we struggle with most. It can feel like rejection or silence, but a "no" from God is often His mercy in disguise. Just like a good parent doesn't say "yes" to everything a child wants, our Heavenly Father says "no" when it protects us, helps us grow, or redirects us toward something better.

The apostle Paul knew this firsthand. He pleaded with God three times to remove the thorn in his flesh, but God said no. Why? Because God's grace was enough, and His power would be made perfect in

Paul's weakness (2 Corinthians 12:7–9). God's "no" was not neglect—it was love.

But sometimes what feels like a "no" is really, "not yet." Waiting tests our trust, stretches our patience, and deepens our dependence. But Scripture is filled with stories of delayed answers that proved to be perfectly timed. Abraham waited decades for his promised son. Joseph waited years in prison before stepping into his calling. Even Jesus waited to begin His public ministry. In each case, the delay wasn't denial—it was preparation. God was aligning circumstances, building character, and shaping history.

If you're in a season of waiting, don't lose heart. Just because God hasn't answered in the way you hoped or as fast as you'd like doesn't mean He isn't working. Sometimes, the delay we dread is the very delay we need, and God knows that better than we do.

In fact, waiting is often where the deepest work of God happens. While we tend to view waiting as wasted time, God uses it to refine us. In the delay, He teaches us perseverance. In the silence, He builds our faith. In the unanswered prayers, He invites us into deeper trust, not just in what He can do, but in who He is.

Delays Aren't Denials

One of the best examples of this is found in John 11. Jesus' dear friend, Lazarus, was sick. His sisters, Mary and Martha, sent word to Jesus, hoping He would come and heal their brother. But Scripture says, "When he heard that Lazarus was sick, he stayed where he was two more days" (John 11:6). It sounds confusing—almost uncaring—but Jesus had something greater in mind. He didn't come immediately.

He didn't say "yes" to their request right away. But He didn't say "no," either. He said "not yet."

When Jesus finally arrived, Lazarus had been dead for four days. It looked like all hope was lost. But then Jesus raised him from the dead, revealing His power not just as a healer, but as The Resurrection and the Life. If Jesus had come earlier, they would have seen a healing. Because He waited, they saw a resurrection.

That's what God does in the "not yet." He prepares us to see something better than what we asked for. My wife keeps a cartoon on her phone that shows a little girl clutching a ragged, well-loved teddy bear in her arms. A thought bubble above her head says, "But I love it, God." Kneeling in front of her is Jesus, gently reaching out His hand. Behind His back, He's holding a much bigger, newer teddy bear. His thought bubble says, "If only you'll trust Me." That image says it all. God's "no" or "not yet" isn't the end of the story—it's often the beginning of something better.

That doesn't mean waiting is easy. Waiting on God can stretch your faith and test your patience. But some of the most important growth in your life will happen not in answered prayer, but in the space between asking and receiving. That's where your roots go deep, and spiritual maturity is formed.

It also gives you the opportunity to build your trust in God. Trust isn't about pretending everything is fine—it's about choosing to believe that God is working even when you can't see it. It's about surrendering your timeline and placing your confidence in God's goodness, even when the outcome is uncertain. Trust says, "Even if I don't understand what You're doing, I know who You are." And that kind of trust doesn't come overnight—it's built one decision at a time in the waiting room of life.

So whatever answer you're living with today—whether it's a joyful "yes," a painful "no," or an agonizing "not yet"—remember that God is still good. He is still listening. And He is still working behind the scenes for your good and His glory.

Your job is to keep praying. Keep believing. Keep trusting. Because the God who hears every prayer also knows the perfect way and the perfect time to answer.

Prayer:
Father, thank You that Your ways are higher than mine. When I don't understand the delays or the denials, help me trust that You are still good, still wise, and still working. Teach me to wait with hope, to surrender with peace, and to keep praying with faith—no matter the outcome. I believe You hear me. I believe You care. Give me the strength to hold on in the waiting and the humility to accept Your "no" when it comes. More than answers, I want You. Shape my heart through every response—yes, no, or not yet. I trust You. In Jesus' name, Amen.

GOD ANSWERS EVERY PRAYER,
BUT NOT ALWAYS IN THE WAY
WE WANT OR EXPECT.

The Tabernacle Prayer

I once heard Pastor Chris Hodges teach on the Tabernacle Prayer. In the Old Testament, the Tabernacle was a special place where God met with His people. It was designed exactly how God instructed, and as people entered, they went through seven different areas to prepare themselves and draw near to Him.

Today, we don't need a physical Tabernacle to be close to God, but those same steps can still help us connect with Him in a meaningful way. This prayer model walks us through each part of the Tabernacle and uses the purpose of each one to guide our time with God through prayer.

1. The Outer Court (Thanksgiving and Praise)
Begin your prayer with thanksgiving and praise, just like the Israelites did. Focus your heart on God's goodness—His love, faithfulness, and provision. Take time to thank Him, sing, write, or reflect quietly. Let gratitude fill your heart as you lift your eyes and honor Him.

2. The Brazen Altar (The Cross of Jesus)
In the Old Testament, sacrifices covered sin, but then Jesus came and paid the ultimate price once and for all. Take a moment to thank Him. Reflect on the cross—His love, your freedom, and forgiveness. Let gratitude fill your heart as you remember what His sacrifice means for your life today.

3. The Laver (Cleansing and Preparing)
At the laver, people stopped to wash and prepare to enter God's presence. Because of Jesus, we can confess our sins and be completely forgiven. Ask God to cleanse your heart, reveal anything needing change, and renew you. Surrender fully, and let this be a moment of spiritual reset.

4. The Candlestick (The Holy Spirit)

The golden candlestick symbolized the Holy Spirit's presence and power. Today, the Holy Spirit is our Helper—guiding, comforting, and empowering us. Ask Him to fill you, lead your day, and help you shine God's light in the world. We can't live for Jesus without His Spirit working in us.

5. The Table of Shewbread (The Word of God)

The table of bread reminded Israel that God's Word is our daily nourishment. Just as food strengthens the body, Scripture strengthens the soul. Spend time reading His Word. Let it speak to your heart and shape your life. God's Word is a vital, powerful part of your prayer journey.

6. The Altar of Incense (Worship)

The altar of incense represented worship rising to God. As you pray, draw near by honoring who He is. Thank Him for His presence and celebrate His Name. Worship brings Him joy and pulls you closer. Let your heart respond with love, not just for what He's done—but for who He is.

7. The Ark of the Covenant (Intercession)

The Holy of Holies (sacred place) reminds us to intercede for others. Just as the priest prayed for the people, we're called to lift up those in need. Pray for family, friends, and anyone hurting. Name them before God. Your prayers matter—intercession brings hope, healing, and invites God to move in power.

PART 3

WHAT HAPPENS WHEN WE SEEK

CHAPTER FIFTEEN

HEARING GOD'S VOICE

"My sheep listen to my voice; I
know them, and they follow me"
- John 10:27

In September 1946, while on a train ride to the Loreto Convent
in Darjeeling for her annual retreat, 36-year-old Mother Teresa
experienced a profound spiritual encounter that would alter the course
of her life. Though she rarely spoke in detail about what happened
during that journey, she later revealed,

"[It] was a call within my vocation. It was a second calling. It was
a vocation to give up even Loreto where I was very happy and
to go out in the streets to serve the poorest of the poor. It was in
that train, I heard the call to give up all and follow Him into the
slums—to serve Him in the poorest of the poor.... I knew it was
His will and that I had to follow Him. There was no doubt that it
was going to be His work."[38]

Until then, she had been faithfully teaching at the Loreto Convent in Calcutta and was content in her ministry. But on that train, she sensed a new and deeper directive from Christ, one that would lead her away from the comfort of convent life and into the streets among those in deepest poverty. She felt clearly and unmistakably that God was asking her to serve Him by caring for the poorest of the poor. That moment marked the birth of what would eventually become the Missionaries of Charity, and the day would later be commemorated by her community as "Inspiration Day."

Her encounter on the train reshaped the rest of her life. Hearing God wasn't a one-time experience. She once said, "in the silence of the heart God speaks."[39]

That kind of listening takes practice. It's how we learn to quiet the world around us and the noise within us. Prayer and fasting clears the space so we can hear Him when He does.

Ears to Hear

Jesus had a saying He used often—"he who has ears to hear, let him hear." He said it because He knew the people who heard Him speak often misunderstood what He was trying to say, and unfortunately, that problem has not gone away.

Many people still struggle with spiritual hearing. We listen to sermons, read Scripture, and even pray, but we don't always recognize when God is trying to speak to us. The idea of "hearing God's voice" can feel confusing or even a little strange. But I believe God is speaking to you and me often, and prayer and fasting are ways we can better attune our hearts to hear what He is saying.

No story shows this more beautifully than Elijah in 1 Kings 19.

Elijah had just come off of a spiritual high. He had called down fire from heaven, defeated the prophets of Baal, and seen God move in undeniable power. But immediately after that victory, he found himself running for his life, exhausted, afraid, and emotionally crushed. He was done. "I have had enough, Lord," he said. "Take my life" (1 Kings 19:4). He didn't want to go on. So what did God do? He didn't scold Elijah. He gently provided food and water through an angel, then allowed Elijah to rest. Next, Elijah fasted for 40 days as he journeyed to Mount Horeb.

When he arrived at Mount Horeb, Elijah experienced a dramatic sequence: a mighty wind, a powerful earthquake, and a blazing fire. But God wasn't in any of those. It's not that he can't be; sometimes He is, but this time, and most times, God's voice came as a gentle whisper. It was in that moment that Elijah pulled his cloak over his face, stepped forward, and listened.

That's what prayer and fasting do. They don't make God speak louder. They turn down the volume of our life so we can hear Him. They tune our ears to the whisper. In that whisper, God didn't just comfort Elijah—He gave him direction. He recommissioned him and laid out the next steps of Elijah's calling.

Take Moses as another example. It was during 40 days of fasting on Mount Sinai that God spoke to him and gave him the laws and commandments for the Israelites. Moses didn't receive that revelation while handling day-to-day leadership burdens. He received it when he was alone with God, fasting and praying on the mountain (Exodus 34).

There seems to be a pattern throughout Scripture: When people pray and fast, and get away from the noise, God draws near and speaks.

In his book, *How to Hear God*, Pete Greig explains three main challenges many of us face when it comes to hearing God's voice in that quiet, conversational way. The challenges are psychological, theological, and experiential.[40]

Psychologically, we often feel unworthy. We wonder, "Why would God speak to someone like me?" We compare ourselves to people in the Bible or leaders we admire, and think we're not spiritual enough to have that kind of connection with God. The truth is, many of us doubt whether we're the kind of person God would actually want to speak to.

Theologically, some of us are unsure whether God still speaks at all. Maybe we've been taught that God only spoke in Bible times and doesn't speak in personal ways anymore. Or maybe we think that because we have the Bible, we don't need anything else. I know some brilliant theology professors who openly admit they do not believe that God speaks—or even that He *can* speak today. Sadly, their brilliance has become a barrier. They can articulate doctrine with precision, yet they don't believe the God of Scripture still reveals Himself in a personal way. But all through Scripture, God is shown as a relational God—One who speaks, listens, and responds. Why would that change now?

Experientially, most of us simply haven't learned how to recognize God's voice. We've never been taught what to listen for, so we don't know what it sounds like. We might expect something dramatic or supernatural, and when that doesn't happen, we assume we didn't hear anything. But like any relationship, learning to truly hear someone takes time and practice.

There's something about the posture of prayer and an empty stomach that helps us hear better. I can't fully explain it, but it's undeniable. It can be a thought that won't go away, part of a conversation that keeps coming up, a verse of scripture that resonates deeply, or a prompting or inclination in your spirit that you just know to be God.

Prayer:

Father, I want to hear You. In a world full of noise and distraction, teach me to be still and listen. Quiet the chaos in my mind and the clutter in my heart. Help me recognize Your voice—not just in the spectacular, but in the silence. Like Elijah, give me ears to hear the whisper. Let fasting sharpen my sensitivity and draw me closer to Your presence. Speak, Lord, even if it's just one word. And when You do, give me the courage to respond with trust and obedience. I'm listening. I'm waiting. I'm Yours. In Jesus' name, Amen.

PRAYER AND FASTING DON'T
MAKE GOD SPEAK LOUDER—
THEY HELP YOU BECOME
QUIET ENOUGH TO HEAR HIM.

The Miracle of Ezekiel Jordan

When Ezekiel Jordan was five days old, the Beltrans got the call that he had tested positive for a neuro muscular disease called SMA (Spinal Muscular Atrophy). SMA is a muscular dystrophy related disease in which a child is born missing the gene that continues to produce motor neurons. When a child has this disease it causes them to lose all function, which in return can render them immobile, and in a lot of cases, result in infant death.

They were devastated. But somehow, at that moment, they knew they had to call on the Lord for healing and guidance. They also knew they needed their church family to start praying and fasting for Ezekiel and his healing.

A few days later, the hospital called to let them know they needed to act fast. Ezekiel needed treatment before he lost his strength. The good news was there was a treatment, the bad news was it cost over $2 million to receive. So, their next prayers were for their insurance company to approve the costly treatment, and they did! They approved it within weeks!

Over the last three years, Ezekiel has shown no signs of SMA. He has beaten and excelled every milestone the doctors used to determine his progress. He is walking, running, talking, eating by himself, and shows no signs of slowing down. He truly is a miracle.

Their final bill from the hospital was $3.2 million, and their insurance company paid every single penny except a $1,200 deductible.

On their last doctor's visit, they asked Ezekiel's doctor, "Do you think Ezekiel will ever lose strength and not walk?" The doctor said, "I think Ezekiel has truly beat SMA, and I wouldn't worry about him ever not walking. God is truly on your side."

They didn't know it when they named him, but Ezekiel means "God strengthens," and that's what He continues to do. The Lord truly is faithful and still performing miracles. They are blessed to be raising one of them.

CHAPTER SIXTEEN

OPEN DOORS

"I know your deeds. See, I have placed before
you an open door that no one can shut…"
- Revelation 3:8

David Brainerd did not have a large platform, but his devotion to prayer, fasting, and the presence of God left a large impact. Born in 1718, Brainerd lived only 29 years, yet his journal has inspired generations of missionaries, pastors, and intercessors. His life is a clear example of how God opens doors through humble, persevering prayer and fasting.

As a young man, Brainerd struggled with depression, poor health, and intense loneliness, but despite these obstacles, he carried a deep burden to reach Native American tribes with the gospel. In his journal, Brainerd often wrote of entire days spent in the woods on his face before God, weeping and interceding. He would fast for extended periods out of desperation for God to move.[41]

For Brainerd, doors didn't swing open easily. He was expelled from Yale due to a theological disagreement with the school's leaders. This should have disqualified him from ministry, but instead, it became the setup for something greater. God opened a different door—an invitation from the Society in Scotland for Propagating Christian Knowledge to serve as a missionary to Native Americans in New England.

Brainerd's work among the Delaware and Susquehanna tribes didn't yield immediate results. For months, he preached with little fruit. But he continued to fast, pray, and plead with God for revival. Then, suddenly and without human explanation, doors began to open. Hearts softened. Entire families turned to Christ. In a short time, hundreds were baptized.

Even after his health failed and he had to return to Jonathan Edwards' home to die, his influence didn't stop. Edwards was so moved by Brainerd's passion and persistence that he published his journal. The resulting book became one of the most influential missionary texts in history, helping launch the modern missions movement and inspiring men like William Carey and Henry Martyn to take the gospel to unreached places.[42]

David Brainerd never saw the full fruit of his faithfulness, but God used his life to open doors around the world. His story reminds us that when you give yourself to seeking God in private, He opens doors in public.

Fasting and the Favor of God

When we talk about "open doors," we mean unexpected opportunities, supernatural favor, or divine appointments we couldn't have orchestrated ourselves—a conversation, a connection, a promotion, a platform, or a breakthrough that God has put in place. And one of the clearest biblical patterns is this: Fasting often precedes favor.

Fasting is about posture. It says to God, "I am not trusting my own ability to make things happen. I'm trusting You!" It's a way of stepping back from striving so we can lean fully into surrender. And when you do that—when you give up something physical to seek something spiritual—God meets you with grace. Often, the result is that He opens doors you couldn't have planned or predicted.

Biblical Patterns of Favor

Take Daniel, for example. In Daniel 1, the young Hebrew men were in Babylon, a foreign land with unfamiliar customs. Rather than compromise their convictions, Daniel and his friends fasted from the royal food and chose a simpler diet. That fast wasn't about show—it was about honor. They wanted to honor God even in captivity. And what happened? "Now God had caused the official to show favor and compassion to Daniel" (Daniel 1:9). Their surrender attracted God's help. By the end of the chapter, Daniel and his friends were not only healthier but "ten times better" than anyone else in the king's service. That's what divine favor looks like: an open door that only God could swing wide.

Esther's story is another powerful example. She was not born into royalty. She was a Jewish exile, plucked from obscurity into a Persian beauty contest. But when the survival of her people was on the line, she didn't act on impulse. She fasted and called others to fast (Esther 4:16), and then she approached the king uninvited—a move punishable by death. But instead of judgment, the king extended his gold scepter and welcomed her. That's favor. Esther fasted and found herself standing in a room she had no business being in, making a request she had no right to make—and it was granted.

Prayer and fasting position us for those moments. They clear our motives, humble our hearts, and make space for God to move.

In the New Testament, we see the same pattern. Jesus began His public ministry with 40 days of prayer and fasting in the wilderness. There were no crowds, no miracles, no followers—just hunger, testing, and obedience. But what followed was astounding: Doors began to fly open. People flocked to hear Him. Miracles began to break out. Demons fled at His word. Favor followed the fast.

Throughout history, we see great moves of God that were preceded by seasons of intercessory prayer and private fasting, including the early church in the book of Acts (1st century), the Moravian prayer movement (1727), the First Great Awakening in America (1730s–40s), the Welsh Revival (1904–1905), and the Azusa Street Revival (1906).

People fasted not to get something from God, but to give more of themselves to Him. And as they did, favor found them—doors opened, influence expanded, and resources grew.

So how does this apply to us? Most of us aren't standing before kings or crossing oceans. But all of us are in need of open doors—doors we cannot open ourselves. You may need favor in a conversation, a job, a decision, a ministry, or your finances. And while God is always working, fasting is a way to posture your heart for His favor.

You don't have to force your way into God's plans. He's the One who opens doors—often in ways we could never predict and at times we least expect. But there's a pattern throughout Scripture and history: When people humble themselves through prayer and fasting, God responds. Hearts shift. Doors open. Favor follows. Trust that even now, God is preparing something ahead of you—an open door, waiting for the right time.

Prayer:

Father, I surrender my plans, my striving, and my timeline to You. I trust that You are the God who opens doors no one can shut. Teach me to wait with faith, to fast with humility, and to pray with boldness. Even when I don't see immediate results, help me believe You are working behind the scenes. Align my heart with Your will, and give me the courage to walk through whatever doors You open. May my life reflect trust, not control—dependence, not pride. Use my prayers and fasting to shape me for Your purpose. In Jesus' name, Amen.

WHEN YOU FAST AND PRAY,
GOD OPENS DOORS NO
ONE CAN CLOSE.

Jonathan's Miracle Story

On March 28, 2025, Jonathan was taken to the emergency room by his wife after experiencing tightness in his chest. While there, doctors discovered that he had colon cancer. In the days that followed, even more devastating news came—Jonathan's cancer had spread to his liver and lymph nodes. It was stage 4 and aggressive. The doctor was not optimistic and warned that he was at risk of liver failure. The diagnosis was shocking and heartbreaking for Jonathan and his family. Within a week, he began to lose weight and feel fatigued as his condition rapidly declined.

Both Jonathan and his wife come from strong Christian families and have raised their children with the same faith. When faced with this overwhelming diagnosis, they immediately turned to prayer. Even when they didn't have the perfect words, they trusted that God knew their need. Together, individually, and with their children, they prayed daily—asking for the right doctor, the best treatment plan, and complete healing. Though the medical reports were grim, they held fast to their belief that with God, all things are possible.

For weeks, they prayed for a word from God—some comfort to calm their hearts. Then one morning, Jonathan had a dream. In it, his grandfather introduced him to a man who shook his hand and said, "The Lord told me you are going through something." When Jonathan explained his situation, the man replied, "The Lord says everything is going to be okay." When

Jonathan woke and shared the dream, the fear lifted. He knew God was in control.

Their church family joined them in prayer. Because of the risk to his liver, chemotherapy began on April 25. That same week, his pastor began a series titled *The God Who Heals*, with the following Sunday designated as Miracle and Healing Sunday. Jonathan and his wife knew immediately that he needed to attend and go through the prayer line. Surrounded by family and friends, he lifted his hands to God during that service and felt the Holy Spirit's presence in a powerful way. That day marked a turning point. His appetite, which had been gone for weeks, returned, and he was able to eat dinner for the first time in a long while.

The chemotherapy treatments were strong and demanding, but in June, they received incredible news—the treatments were working. The scans showed a reduction in tumor size and the cancer's burden on his liver. By September, after eight treatments, another scan revealed significant improvement. The cancer was almost gone, and the doctor called it "the best possible outcome." For Jonathan and his family, it was more than good news—it was confirmation that God was still at work.

Although Jonathan is still walking through this journey, he has now transitioned from chemotherapy to oral medication. He and his family remain steadfast in faith and prayer, trusting that this season will soon come to an end. Through it all, Jonathan has learned that prayer and fasting truly invite God's presence and power. He stands as living proof that the Lord still heals, still works miracles, and is the same yesterday, today, and forever.

CHAPTER SEVENTEEN

KNOWING GOD'S WILL

"While they were worshiping the Lord and fasting,
the Holy Spirit said, 'Set apart for me Barnabas and
Saul for the work to which I have called them.'"
- Acts 13:2

William Carey is often remembered as the "father of modern missions," a title he never sought, but rightly earned. But what many don't realize is that before Carey ever stepped foot on Indian soil, he spent years wrestling in prayer and fasting, seeking clarity about God's will.

Carey was a shoemaker in England with a brilliant mind and a burning heart for the nations. While repairing shoes and reading Scripture, he became burdened by the reality that millions around the world had never heard the gospel. At the time, most churches in England were inwardly focused, with little vision for global evangelism. Missionary work was rare and considered unnecessary by many.

But Carey couldn't shake the burden. He read the writings of early missionaries, pored over maps, and compiled statistics on unreached people groups. The more he studied, the more convinced he became that God was calling him to go. But clarity didn't come overnight.[43]

In 1784, Carey and a group of friends set aside the second Tuesday of every month to fast and pray for "the revival of real religion, and the extension of Christ's kingdom in the world."[44]For eight years, the men met, fasted, and prayed together every month. Then in 1793, Carey sailed to India and spent the rest of his life as a missionary. He never returned to his homeland.

Today, William Carey's legacy lives on through thousands of missionaries and countless people reached with the gospel. His story is a powerful reminder that when we humble ourselves, fast, and pray, God will guide our steps.

Straight Paths

Everyone wants a clear direction for their life. We want to know: What is God's will? What should I do next? Should I take this job? Pursue this relationship? Make this move? These are real and honest questions, and God is not silent in response. In fact, He delights in guiding His people. The Bible says, "your ears will hear a voice behind you, saying, 'This is the way, walk in it'" (Isaiah 30:21). God promises clarity, but it often comes only when we've made space to listen.

Prayer and fasting tune our hearts to hear the voice of God. They quiet our inner world. We live in a culture of noise, with constant opinions, information, and stimulation. Even good things can cloud our ability to hear from heaven. Fasting removes distractions, both physical and spiritual. It trains us to be still, to wait, and to recognize the whispers of the Holy Spirit that are often drowned out by daily life.

We see a beautiful example of this in Acts 13. The early church was gathered in worship, prayer, and fasting, and "the Holy Spirit said, 'Set apart for me Barnabas and Saul for the work to which I have called them.'" God spoke to people while they were praying and fasting, and as a result, Paul and Barnabas were sent on what became the first missionary journey. The global spread of the gospel was fueled by people who were committed to prayer and fasting.

God still works like that. He still leads those who are seeking, and He still provides clarity to the humble heart that makes space to hear. Disciplines like prayer and fasting say, "God, I'm serious about hearing from You. I'm willing to set aside my comfort to pursue Your voice." This is the pattern: humility, prayer, fasting, and then clarity.

If you're in a season of decision-making, uncertainty, or waiting, fasting is a powerful way to seek the Lord. You may not get an audible voice or a flashing sign, but you may receive a settled peace, a fresh insight from Scripture, a confirming word from a friend, or a sudden clarity in your spirit, because God leads those who are searching for Him.

In Proverbs 3:5–6, we are given one of the most well-known and comforting promises in Scripture: "Trust in the Lord with all your heart and lean not on your own understanding; in all your ways submit to Him, and He will make your paths straight." That's what spiritual disciplines do—clear away our limited understanding and help us acknowledge God in every area of our lives.

The stories of William Carey and the early church in Acts remind us that God's guidance is not reserved for a select few. God still speaks to ordinary people who are willing to seek Him with extraordinary devotion.

Prayer and fasting can help us align with God's heart in seasons of transition, uncertainty, or longing for purpose. It's less about getting what we want and more about becoming the kind of person who wants what God wants. That's the real gift of guidance—not just a map for the future, but a heart aligned with God's will.

If you feel stuck, confused, or desperate for direction, there's no better practice than to fast and pray. God's will isn't just something to discover—it's something to desire. So turn down the noise, step away from distractions, and give God your undivided attention. He will guide you. He will speak. He will make your path straight.

Prayer:
Father, I surrender my plans and desires to You. I don't want to rush ahead or lag behind—I want to walk in step with Your Spirit. As I fast and seek Your face, tune my heart to hear Your voice. Silence the noise within and around me so I can recognize Your leading. Give me wisdom for each decision and peace to trust You even when the path is unclear. Help me to wait on You. I believe You will guide me. Open the doors You've prepared, and make my path straight. In Jesus' name, Amen.

PRAYER AND FASTING
AREN'T ABOUT GETTING
OUR WAY–THEY'RE ABOUT
WANTING GOD'S WAY.

Hunter's Story of Rescue and Redemption

Warning: This story contains graphic details of a suicide attempt.

November 19, 2024, is a date Ryan and Jaime will never forget. For months, their son Hunter had been slipping further into a world of lies, depression, and darkness. They tried everything, but nothing seemed to reach him. Night after night, they prayed, pleading with God to rescue their son. But from their perspective, nothing was changing.

That evening in November, a loud sound echoed from the basement. Ryan rushed downstairs and was met with a moment no parent should ever experience. There, with tears streaming down his face, Hunter looked up and said the unthinkable: "I tried to kill myself."

The days that followed were unbearable. Hunter was admitted to a mental health facility—18 years old, broken, and deeply afraid. Visitors weren't allowed. All they could do was send messages and wait and pray from a distance. But even in that darkness, God was at work.

A staff member from their church suggested that Hunter ask for a Bible. To everyone's surprise, he agreed. And as he began to read, his faith began to be stirred. Friends, family, and pastors started sending Bible verses and words of hope, identity, and healing. His faith was growing.

Weeks later, Hunter admitted that right before he lost consciousness in the basement, he whispered a desperate prayer: "God, save me." In that moment, the neck tie around his neck snapped. He couldn't explain how—it just did.

That miraculous moment became a turning point. Ryan, Jaime, and his sister, Peyton, found themselves praying and fasting day in and day out, along with the overwhelming support from their pastors and church family. Their church surrounded them, prayed with them, and many committed to fasting for Hunter—to be healed, saved, and set free.

After leaving the facility, Hunter fully surrendered his life to Christ. Not long after, he was baptized. Today, he continues to follow Jesus with courage, purpose, and gratitude—living proof that even in our darkest moments, God is still writing stories of redemption.

CHAPTER EIGHTEEN

BREAKING STRONGHOLDS

"He told them, 'Because of your lack of faith. I tell all of you
with certainty, if you have faith like a grain of mustard seed,
you can say to this mountain, "Move from here to there," and
it will move, and nothing will be impossible for you. But this
kind does not come out except by prayer and fasting.'"
- Matthew 17:20–21 (ISV)

David Wilkerson was a young country pastor with a burden for
something more. Feeling prompted by God, he stopped watching
television in the evening and started praying at that time instead. This
small act of devotion quickly led him into deeper seasons of fasting and
intercession. Night after night, he prayed alone in his study, sensing
that God was preparing him for something he didn't yet understand.

During one of these fasts, David saw a photo in Life Magazine of
seven alleged teenage gang members on trial for murder in New York
City, and something gripped his spirit. He couldn't explain it—he just
knew he had to go. So he left his small Pennsylvania town and drove
into the heart of gang territory in New York City, armed with nothing
but holy conviction.

The result of that simple fast led to something no one would have
predicted: Teen Challenge, a ministry that has helped thousands find
freedom from addiction, abuse, and gang life through the love of Jesus

Christ. But it all started with a secret hunger and desire for something more. Wilkerson would later write, "Your present struggle may be the breaking point heaven is waiting for. Strongholds don't break casually. They break when you choose hunger for God over comfort."[45]

What Is A Stronghold

There are some battles in life that can't be won with willpower alone. Some habits won't break with effort alone. Some chains won't fall with prayer alone. According to Jesus, some strongholds require prayer and fasting.

So, what is a stronghold? Think of a stronghold like a mental or emotional prison. You may be free in Christ, but this area of your life feels locked up. You may love Jesus, but there's this one issue that keeps coming back. Something in your thoughts, your identity, your emotions, or your behavior just won't let go—and nothing you've tried has broken it. It can be a deeply held lie, mindset, or attitude that resists the truth of God and holds you captive in some area of your life.

Some common strongholds include fear that controls your decisions; addiction that keeps returning despite your efforts; lies about your worth, value, or identity; bitterness or unforgiveness that poisons relationships; shame from your past that still defines you; or doubt that keeps you from believing God's promises.

Strongholds are built by repeated thoughts and reinforced by past wounds, trauma, sin, and spiritual deception. Over time, they become areas where the enemy whispers, "God can't change this," or "This is just who you are now." Tragically, many people start to believe those lies.

That's what makes strongholds so powerful—they don't just affect what we do; they affect what we believe. But here's the good news: strongholds can be torn down. And prayer and fasting are two of the most powerful spiritual weapons we have.

Why? Because these disciplines interrupt patterns. They humble the flesh and open the door for truth to get in. When you pray and fast, you are saying, "God, I want You more than I want this comfort, this addiction, this lie." You're breaking your agreement with the stronghold and choosing to align with God's Word instead.

Strongholds are broken when lies are replaced with truth, and prayer and fasting help you see those lies more clearly and receive God's truth more fully.

You don't have to be stuck. The stronghold doesn't have to win. You're not too far gone. When you fast and pray, you're not just starving your flesh—you're feeding your faith and inviting the power of God to do what your willpower never could.

Fasting for Freedom

In Matthew 17, a desperate father brought his demon-possessed son to Jesus. The boy was suffering greatly, and the father pleaded for help. He had gone to the disciples first, and even though they had previously cast out demons and healed the sick, this time, they had failed.

Jesus rebuked the demon, healed the boy, and restored peace to the family. Later, the disciples asked Him privately, "Why couldn't we drive it out?" Jesus replied, "Because of your lack of faith... but this kind does not come out except by prayer and fasting."

The lesson here is important: *Not all spiritual resistance is the same.* Some battles are heavier. Some addictions are more stubborn. Some bondages go deeper. And sometimes, prayer alone isn't enough. We need the focused, sacrificial power of fasting to break through. Jesus was saying, "You can't do what I do publicly because you refuse to do what I do privately."

Fasting weakens the flesh so the Spirit can lead. It brings clarity, sharpens faith, and increases authority. But it's not that fasting makes us more powerful in ourselves—rather, it draws us deeper into dependence on the One who has all the power. When we fast, we align our hearts with God's strength, not our own.

Strongholds aren't just bad habits—they're spiritual grip points the enemy uses to hold us back from freedom. Fasting disrupts the cycle. It breaks the agreement we've unknowingly made with our bondage and invites God's authority to take over.

You may not even know what kind of stronghold you're facing until you start fasting. But as your flesh is quieted and your spirit is awakened, things begin to shift. The pull of the addiction weakens. The lie you've believed gets exposed. The anger you've carried begins to soften.

And sometimes, when we've prayed all we know how to pray, when we've read Scripture and still feel stuck, when we've asked for help but can't seem to change, Jesus' words still stand: "But this kind does not come out except by prayer and fasting."

In 2 Corinthians 10:4, Paul writes, "The weapons we fight with are not the weapons of the world. On the contrary, they have divine power to demolish strongholds." That word—demolish—isn't passive. It's not about managing the stronghold, hiding it better, or learning to live with it. It's about tearing it down completely, brick by brick, until there's nothing left to stand between you and the freedom Jesus died to give you.

That's what fasting does. It doesn't just weaken your flesh—it strengthens your spirit. It creates space in your heart and mind for the Holy Spirit to shine a spotlight on the lies you've believed, and to replace them with truth.

Maybe you've assumed you'll always struggle with anxiety. Maybe you've accepted that lust is just part of your story. Maybe you believe your family's history of addiction, divorce, or depression will always define your future. But those are lies!

You don't have to live under the weight of a stronghold forever. What's been hidden can be revealed. What's been stuck can be released. What's been too strong for you is not too strong for God.

The enemy wants you to believe you'll always be stuck. But God wants you to know *this kind can come out*. Not by willpower, not by guilt, and not by shame, but by prayer and fasting.

Prayer:
Father, I come to You with humility, acknowledging the strongholds in my life—those places where I feel stuck, bound, or weary from the fight. Thank You that freedom is possible through the power of Jesus. As I fast and pray, tear down every lie I've believed and replace it with Your truth. Strengthen my spirit, quiet my flesh, and help me hear Your voice clearly. I trust that what I cannot break, You can demolish. I believe You are greater than my struggle. Set me free, Lord, and lead me into the fullness of the freedom You've promised. In Jesus' name, Amen.

FASTING DOESN'T JUST WEAKEN YOUR FLESH—IT STRENGTHENS YOUR SPIRIT.

Amana's Prayer

During 21 days of prayer and fasting with their church, Joseph and Christa began to feel a strong urge to pray to have another child. It had been seven years since they were blessed with their first and only child, Amana, and infertility had caused them to doubt whether having another child was part of God's will for their life.

Their pastor declared Psalm 77:14, "You are the God who performs miracles; you display your power among the people." This verse began to burn within our hearts, but unexpectedly their daughter, Amana began praying for a sibling too. Every morning, during 21 days of prayer and fasting, their little girl would march up to the altar, grab a prayer card, and write down the same request for a sibling. Her extreme persistence began to stir her family's faith.

One day, they confessed out loud their desire for a child to their small group. It was the first time they had shared it publicly. Their friends joined them in agreement believing God would grow their family.

Toward the end of the 21 days, Amana became adamant that God had given her a dream that her mommy was pregnant. Some people tried to minimize her dream, assuming it was a little girl being excited, but they couldn't diminish her faith. Amana was right! Joseph and Christa's new son, Jotham Roland Ayers was born 9 months later. God answered their prayers.

CHAPTER NINETEEN

ANSWERED PRAYERS

"So we fasted and petitioned our God
about this, and he answered our prayer."
- Ezra 8:23

During the height of the Cold War, when communist regimes banned the Bible and persecuted Christians, Brother Andrew dared to do the unthinkable, smuggling Bibles across heavily guarded borders. His mission was simple but dangerous: Deliver God's word to believers who had no access to Scripture.

In 1957, on one of his early trips into Yugoslavia, Brother Andrew approached the border in a Volkswagen Beetle filled with illegal Bibles. The guards at these borders were notorious for their inspections—taking cars apart piece by piece in search of banned materials. Other drivers were being pulled out, interrogated, and searched. Brother Andrew knew what was at stake. If caught, he faced arrest, imprisonment, or worse. But he also knew the power of prayer.

As he inched forward in the inspection line, he whispered a bold and specific prayer:

"Lord, in my luggage I have Scripture I want to take to Your children across this border. When You were on earth, You made blind eyes see. Now, I pray, make seeing eyes blind. Do not let the guards see those things You do not want them to see."[46]

There was no time for clever hiding or deception. He had placed the Bibles right on the seat next to him—the guards would find them instantly if they looked in the car. But Andrew believed that God was more powerful than the border patrol.

When his turn came, a soldier motioned him forward, and Brother Andrew rolled down his window. The guard looked inside, glanced around the car, and then waved him through. He didn't search. He didn't ask questions. He didn't even blink. He just moved on to the next vehicle.

Brother Andrew sat there, stunned but grateful. He had just witnessed God answer his prayer in real time. That crossing became the first of many. Over the years, Brother Andrew smuggled millions of Bibles into closed countries—sometimes by car, sometimes by train, sometimes even on foot. He became known as "God's Smuggler," and his story has inspired believers around the world.

His life reminds us that prayer moves obstacles, shifts circumstances, and opens doors. It doesn't always work the way we want or when we want, but it always works in God's time and for God's purpose.

Heaven's Multiplier

In Scripture, prayer and fasting are often linked in moments of deep need or divine direction. Moses fasted and prayed for 40 days as he received the law of God. Esther called for a fast when her people were under threat and needed divine intervention. Nehemiah fasted and prayed before rebuilding the wall. Remember, while we don't pray and fast to manipulate God, we do pray and fast when we have a great need in our lives that requires a miracle.

You can certainly pray without fasting, and you can fast without praying, but there is something about pairing these two disciplines together for maximum impact. Fasting and praying together creates a spiritual multiplier effect. Prayer connects you to God, and fasting disconnects you from the world. Fasting brings urgency and intensity to your prayers. It humbles the flesh and tunes your soul. It reminds you that you are not in control, and that's precisely why you need God.

That's what happened in Ezra 8. The people of Israel were preparing to return from exile and journey back to Jerusalem. It was a long and dangerous road, filled with the threat of ambush and attack. Ezra was leading thousands of people, including women and children, through enemy territory, and they needed God's protection.

He could have asked the king for a military escort, and no one would've blamed him. But instead, Ezra turned to God. He proclaimed a fast and called the people to humble themselves, pray, and seek the Lord. And the Bible says, "He answered our prayer." God responded to their humility with protection, guidance, and provision.

We all have certain needs we can't meet on our own. Fasting and prayer invite God into those impossible places. They are acts of surrender that say, "God, I can't fix this, but I believe You can." Sometimes we keep pushing, striving, and worrying—trying to control outcomes that are beyond our reach. But fasting helps interrupt that cycle. It reminds you that you're not the source of your own strength. It brings you back to a posture of dependency and reminds your spirit: God is my provider. God is my defender. God is my help.

Prayer and fasting open the door for God to do what only He can do, just like they did for Brother Andrew, Ezra, and Esther.

When Ezra called the people to fast and pray, he knew their journey was impossible without divine help. In the same way, we fast because we recognize that there are battles in our lives we can't win on our own.

The world tells us to hustle harder, to rely on ourselves, to push through. But the way of the Kingdom is upside down. Jesus said, "Blessed are the poor in spirit, for theirs is the kingdom of heaven" (Matthew 5:3). When we fast and pray, we're choosing that posture—poor in spirit, and desperate for His presence and power.

And here's what's amazing: God loves to meet us in those moments. He honors our hunger. He hears our prayers. He draws near. He moves. Sometimes He moves by changing our circumstances. Sometimes He moves by changing us. But either way, we are never the same after a season of intentional prayer and fasting.

Whatever you're facing today, bring it before God with fasting and prayer. You may find that what feels like your greatest battle becomes the stage for your greatest breakthrough. The God who shielded Brother Andrew, the God who protected Ezra, the God who rescued Esther's people—that same God sees your need today. And He still moves in response to humble, desperate, faith-filled people.

Prayer:

Father, I bring You the impossible things—the fears I carry, the battles I can't win, and the needs I can't meet on my own. Like Ezra, I humble myself before You in fasting and prayer. I acknowledge that without You, I am lost. But with You, all things are possible. You are still the God of deliverance, the God who hears, and the God who acts. Strengthen my faith, sharpen my focus, and move in power. Let this be a moment where You do what only You can do— for Your glory and my good. In Jesus' name, Amen.

SOMETIMES PRAYER CHANGES OUR CIRCUMSTANCES, BUT PRAYER ALWAYS CHANGES US.

Marlene's Miracle

Marlene was a nurse at a nursing home in 2020 when the COVID-19 virus struck the facility with ferocity. Eventually eight lives would be lost. On May 12, 2020, Marlene contracted an early, potent first variant of COVID-19. Initially, she experienced the typical symptoms, but because of her history of asthma, her condition began to decline rapidly. Within a couple of days, she was experiencing severe breathing difficulties and nearly passed out with dangerously low O_2 saturation levels. Her doctor advised immediate emergency care.

She was admitted to the hospital on a Friday, where she would spend the next 17 days. Each day her family received phone calls from doctors delivering more bad news, saying that everything they were trying was having little or no effect. Eventually, Marlene was intubated with a ventilator and feeding tube in the ICU. As her condition worsened further—developing double pneumonia and blood clots—she was placed on the list for what was considered the last available treatment option: an ECMO machine.

During this time, Marlene's church family surrounded her with prayer and fasting, and love for her family. Her church organized a prayer vigil in the parking lot of the hospital, lifting their voices in bold prayers of faith and declaring healing and deliverance from COVID. They didn't know it but her unit was facing the very parking lot where they prayed.

The very next day, Marlene's family received a call with good news: she had stopped declining and was beginning to recover. From then on, each phone call brought more positive updates. Within days, doctors removed the ventilator and brought her back to consciousness. The medical staff were astonished—the team had not expected Marlene to live much longer and were preparing for the worst. But God had other plans. After 17 days, Marlene was healed and released to go home.

CHAPTER TWENTY

EXPERIENCING REVIVAL

"If my people, who are called by my name, will
humble themselves and pray and seek my face and turn
from their wicked ways, then I will hear from heaven,
and I will forgive their sin and will heal their land."
- 2 Chronicles 7:14

The Hebrides Revival was one of the most remarkable spiritual awakenings of the 20th century, and it all began with two elderly women who knew the power of prayer and fasting.

In the late 1940s, the Isle of Lewis, a remote island in the Hebrides of Scotland, was spiritually dry. Church attendance was declining, and young people were disengaged from faith. The moral and spiritual condition of the island burdened two sisters, Peggy Smith, who was 84 and blind, and her sister, Christine, who was 82 and had arthritis. Though physically frail, they were spiritual giants. They believed that God could bring revival, and they made it their mission to intercede on behalf of others.

Night after night, Peggy and Christine fasted and prayed in their small cottage in the village of Barvas. Their prayers were focused and intense: "Lord, revive your church and send awakening to our young people." They claimed the promise of Isaiah 44:3—"I will pour water on the thirsty land, and streams on the dry ground." And they would not let go.

As they prayed, God gave Peggy a vision. She saw the churches of Lewis crowded with young people, and she became convinced that revival was coming. The sisters sent for their local pastor and urged him to call others to pray as well. A group of church leaders began meeting in a barn to fast and pray two nights a week, seeking God in repentance and humility.[47]

One night, a young man stood and read from Psalm 24: "Who shall ascend the hill of the Lord? He who has clean hands and a pure heart." He cried out, "Are my hands clean? Is my heart pure?" In that moment, the Spirit of God fell on the barn, and the revival began.[48]

Soon after, the famed evangelist Duncan Campbell was invited to preach on the island. At first, he was hesitant, but God redirected his plans. On the first night of his visit, the church building was packed. After the service ended around 11 p.m., people were still hungry for God, and as Campbell and the elders left, they found the streets filled with hundreds of people on their knees, crying out for mercy. The Holy Spirit had swept through the town with no advertising and no fanfare.

What followed over the next three years was a sovereign move of God. Meetings would go on until early morning hours. People walking down the street would be struck by the presence of God and fall to their knees. The young people who were previously hardened to spiritual things wept in repentance. Whole communities were transformed. And it all began with two elderly sisters who believed that God still answers the desperate, humble prayers of His people.

The Hebrides Revival is a powerful reminder that when God's people fast and pray with faith and a pure heart, heaven responds.

Desperate for a Move of God

Desperation is often the doorway to awakening. When people recognize their spiritual poverty and cry out for God with fasting, repentance, and fervent prayer, something shifts in the spiritual atmosphere. That's exactly what 2 Chronicles 7:14 promises. Revival doesn't start in the world—it starts in the church. "If my people... will humble themselves and pray and seek my face and turn from their wicked ways, then I will hear from heaven, and I will forgive their sin and will heal their land."

Fasting plays a vital role in this process. It is a physical expression of a spiritual hunger. It says, "God, we need You more than we need comfort. We're not satisfied with business as usual." Fasting breaks up the hardened soil of complacency and apathy. It weakens the flesh so the Spirit can speak clearly. It brings us to a place of humility, dependence, and fresh surrender. And when prayer and fasting are combined, they become a powerful cry that reaches heaven.

In Joel 2, God calls His people to return with fasting, weeping, and mourning. He says, "Blow the trumpet... declare a holy fast, call a sacred assembly." Why? Because God longs to "pour out His Spirit on all people." Fasting and prayer prepare us for that outpouring.

The Hebrides wasn't the only place to experience this. In the First and Second Great Awakenings in America, revivals were marked by seasons of prayer, fasting, and deep conviction. During the revival in Wales in 1904, churches were packed every night—not because of advertisements, but because people were drawn by the Holy Spirit. In Uganda, South Korea, and Argentina, revival movements have been ignited and sustained through united prayer and fasting.

These awakenings all share a common thread: Public revivals begin in private, with someone who weeps, fasts, prays, and refuses to quit until heaven comes down.

Today, we face many of the same conditions that existed in the Hebrides—spiritual dryness, moral decline, and disinterest in the things of God. But God has not changed. His arm is not too short to save, and His ear is not too dull to hear. He is still looking for people like Peggy and Christine Smith—people who will kneel in secret and believe in public transformation.

Too often, revival is something we wait for. But Scripture and history show us that revival is something we prepare for. It's not a random event; it's a response from heaven to hearts that are desperate, hungry, and surrendered.

Revival doesn't just come to churches—it comes to bedrooms, kitchens, and quiet corners where people cry out to God with everything they have. So do you have a city, church, or family that needs to be revived by a fresh move of God? The easiest thing to do is to complain, but the most effective thing to do is to consecrate yourself through prayer and fasting.

Revival isn't magic. Revival is simply what happens when God's people take their pursuit of Him seriously. When we humble ourselves, fast, pray, and repent, God moves.

Prayer:

Father, we are desperate for You. Our world is weary, our hearts are heavy, and our churches need awakening. So we humble ourselves before You in fasting and prayer. Break up the hardness in us. Stir fresh hunger where apathy has crept in. Cleanse us, revive us, and pour out Your Spirit. Just as You moved in the Hebrides and throughout history, move again in our day. Let our private pursuit lead to public transformation. Make us people who prepare the way for revival. We don't want more religion—we want more of You. Start the awakening in us, Lord. In Jesus' name, Amen.

EVERY PUBLIC REVIVAL
BEGINS WITH SOMEONE
WHO PRAYS IN PRIVATE.

Waiting for Sadie's Miracle

One morning, Jason's daughter Sadie, woke up with a small bump on her tongue. It looked like a minor sore—something they assumed would go away in a few days. But it didn't. Instead, the bump grew larger over the next few weeks until it became a sizable cyst that affected her speech and caused bleeding in her mouth.

Concerned, they took her to the doctor, hoping for a solution. But the news wasn't good. The doctor confirmed it was a cyst and explained that the only possible remedy was a complicated, expensive surgery—and even then, there was no guarantee it would work due to the cyst's location on her tongue.

Jason and his wife were willing to do whatever it took to help their daughter, but the doctor hadn't given them much confidence in the procedure, so they decided to try something else. Jason committed to a 21-day fast—no food, only water—asking God for a miracle. He wanted his daughter to be healed, to live a normal childhood, free from pain. Family members and friends joined in prayer and fasting with him. Every night, they would tuck their daughter into bed and pray together for God to do a miracle.

The way Jason described it, "My faith was sky high. There was no doubt in my mind that God was going to heal my daughter because I was doing something so sacrificial." But as we've already discussed, that's not how fasting works. God doesn't owe us a miracle because we sacrifice for him.

The 21 days came and went—and the cyst remained. In fact, it had grown larger. Jason was crushed. He hadn't eaten in three weeks. He had prayed with all the faith he could muster. Still, there was no breakthrough. Jason was so discouraged. He couldn't understand how God could ignore the prayers and sacrifices of so many other people.

Three months went by, and Jason had stopped praying altogether. They decided to schedule the surgery and hope for the best, but before the surgery happened, God did something miraculous. On a Saturday morning, Jason heard someone running and screaming down the steps. It was Sadie, and she was saying, "Dad, my cyst is gone! My cyst is gone!" She stuck out her tongue and, where there had been a golf-ball-sized lump, there was now no trace of anything. And almost ten years later, it has never returned.

Jason admitted, "Honestly, I had given up all hope that God would heal her. I was just thinking, How am I going to afford this surgery?" He assumed because God didn't answer his prayer in his timeline, God wasn't going to answer his prayer at all. But that's not how prayer works, and that's not how God works. He hears us when we cry out to him, and he answers. Not always how or when we expect, but always at just the right time.

CHAPTER TWENTY-ONE

GREATER INTIMACY

"Come near to God and he will come near to you…"
- James 4:8

John Wesley, the founder of the Methodist movement, was deeply committed to spiritual disciplines. He believed that holiness of heart and life could not be cultivated without regular practices that focused the soul on God. Among these, prayer and fasting held a special place in Wesley's life—not as a legalistic burden, but as a means of grace that opened the heart to deeper fellowship with Christ.

Wesley fasted every Wednesday and Friday from sunup to mid-afternoon, a pattern he adopted early in his ministry and maintained for much of his life.[49] He viewed fasting as a biblical practice, rooted in both the Old and New Testaments, and essential for anyone pursuing a serious walk with God. In fact, Wesley went so far as to say he would not ordain anyone to ministry who was unwilling to fast regularly, believing it to be vital for cultivating humility, dependence on God, and spiritual power.

But for Wesley, fasting was never about earning favor with God.

He was clear that no spiritual discipline could substitute for saving faith in Christ. Instead, he taught that these practices helped create space for God to work more fully in a person's life. Fasting, in his view, was a way of humbling the body so the soul could rise.[50] It was about denying lesser things to make room for the greatest thing: communion with God.

He Draws Near

In this section we've spent a lot of time discussing the results and powerful benefits of prayer and fasting, including hearing God's voice, knowing His will, and experiencing revival. But I've saved the best for last. While prayer and fasting can open doors, bring breakthrough, and lead to miracles—their greatest gift isn't what they change around you, but what they awaken within you.

Fasting and prayer are not just tools to get things from God; ultimately, they're invitations to get closer to Him. While many people fast to seek answers, breakthroughs, or guidance—and those are valid and biblical reasons—one of the greatest results of fasting is intimacy with God Himself. In James 4:8 (ESV), we're given a beautiful promise: "Draw near to God, and he will draw near to you." Fasting is a tangible way we draw near. We're telling our stomach, our schedule, and our senses, "Be still. I'm after something more." And God honors that pursuit. He doesn't play hard to get. When you intentionally move toward Him, He moves toward you. As A.W. Tozer reminds us, "Our pursuit of God is successful just because He is forever seeking to manifest Himself to us."[51]

We see this illustrated in the life of Jesus. Luke 5:16 tells us, "But Jesus often withdrew to lonely places and prayed." The Son of God, who was always full of the Spirit, still prioritized time alone with the Father. He fasted. He prayed. He pulled away from crowds and distractions—not because He lacked anything, but because intimacy with the Father was His highest priority. If Jesus needed that time, how much more do we?

The practice of these spiritual disciplines breaks our selfish routine. It disrupts the normal rhythm of life and creates space to seek, and that space becomes a holy meeting place. You'll start to notice a softness in your heart, a quicker awareness of His presence, and a hunger that goes beyond food.

David wrote in Psalm 63:1, "You, God, are my God, earnestly I seek you; I thirst for you, my whole being longs for you." Fasting and prayer awaken this kind of longing. They reorder our appetites. They teach us to crave God more than comfort, more than success, more than clarity. And here's the beauty: When you make space for God, He fills it.

Many people fast for results, and God does respond, but the most precious result is His nearness. You begin to hear His whispers. His Word feels more alive. Your worship feels more sincere.

Moses spent 40 days on the mountain with God, and when he came down, his face literally glowed. He wasn't seeking a glow—he was seeking God. But intimacy left its mark. It always does. When you spend time with God, especially in a focused season of fasting and prayer, people begin to notice. Your words carry more peace. Your presence sheds more light. Your life reflects His image a little more clearly.

So don't pray and fast just to get something from God. Fast to get *more* of God. Use this time to deepen your friendship with Him. Read His Word slowly. Listen more than you talk. Worship even when you don't feel anything. Show up day after day with a posture that says, "God, I just want to be with You." Because in the end, intimacy with God is the greatest reward. And when your fast is over, you'll find something even better than answers—you'll find Him. And that will always be enough.

Prayer:

Father, I long to know You more. Not just for answers or blessings, but for deeper friendship with You. As I fast and pray, draw near to me. Quiet the noise in my heart. Strip away distractions and awaken a fresh hunger for Your presence. Teach me to love Your Word, to delight in Your nearness, and to listen for Your voice. Like Moses on the mountain and David in the wilderness, let my soul thirst for You above all else. Shape me in the secret place, and let intimacy with You become my highest pursuit. In Jesus' name, Amen.

THE GREATEST REWARD OF FASTING ISN'T RESULTS—IT'S A DEEPER RELATIONSHIP WITH GOD.

A Marriage in God's Hands

After 20 years of marriage, Eddie began to pull away from his wife, his faith, and everything he once valued. Eventually, he asked his wife for a divorce.

The decision seemed so clear in his mind, and nothing his wife said could reach him. In early August, he packed his bags and left for good. He walked out the door, leaving behind his wife and family, and stepped into what he thought was a better life.

Eddie was gone for nine months, but during that time, his wife never stopped praying. She fasted. She worshipped. She cried. And she surrendered. She didn't chase after Eddie—she chased after God. She placed their broken marriage in His hands and trusted Him to do what only He could do.

While his wife continued to pray, Eddie began to feel unsettled. The relationship he had run to wasn't as satisfying as he thought it would be. One day, he finally broke, and he cried out to God.

Eddie immediately got in his car, weeping as he drove home. He was overwhelmed by the pain he had caused. But when he walked through the door, he was met by grace. Eddie's wife was standing there with her arms open. She held him as he wept, and said words he'll never forget: "I'm glad you're home."

Since that day, their marriage has been transformed. It's stronger, deeper, and more joyful than ever. They pray together, worship together, and serve together. They're rebuilding their marriage on a foundation of faith!

IT'S YOUR TURN

"One thing I ask from the Lord, this only do I
seek: that I may dwell in the house of the Lord
all the days of my life, to gaze on the beauty of
the Lord and to seek him in his temple."
- Psalm 27:4

Throughout this book, we've explored the principles and power of prayer and fasting.

From the stories of Esther, Daniel, Ezra, and Jesus, to the revivals in the Hebrides and the passion of men like William Carey and John Wesley, one thread runs through it all: hunger. Not physical hunger, but a deep spiritual hunger that refuses to settle for less than the fullness of God.

Let me share one more story with you. Charles Finney, known as the "Father of Modern Revivalism," was one of the most influential evangelists of the 19th century. A former lawyer turned preacher, he burned with a passion to see lives changed and entire cities transformed by the presence of God. But what most people didn't know was that at the heart of many of Finney's revival meetings was another man named Daniel Nash. He would go into towns days or even weeks before Finney arrived, and pray and fast for God to move.[52]

Nash was a former pastor who, after losing his pulpit due to illness, felt a renewed call—not to preach, but to pray. He would rent a small room, gather a few other prayer warriors, and go to war in the spiritual realm. Sometimes Nash would spend days without speaking to anyone, fasting and praying with groans and tears.

The results were staggering. In city after city, thousands came to Christ. In Rochester, New York, it's estimated that nearly 100,000 people were converted in a single move of God.

Importantly, Nash never tried to take credit. He lived by the principle that those who bend their knees in secret can shape history in public. Daniel Nash died quietly at age 56, and was buried in an unmarked grave in upstate New York. His tombstone reads simply: "Laborer with Finney. Mighty in Prayer."[53]

As I end this book I hope you know by now that prayer and fasting changes things—often circumstances, but always you.

If God could use a blind woman in the Hebrides, a shoemaker in England, and a praying man in a rented room in New York, He can use you. You may never know on this side of heaven what your fasting and prayers accomplished—but rest assured, they matter. Heaven listens, hell trembles, and history shifts when God's people seek Him with all their hearts.

For more resources and information about prayer and fasting, or to contact the author, purchase bulk copies, or inquire about speaking engagements, email contact@deeper21.com

ABOUT THE AUTHOR

J.C. is passionately in love with Jesus! For many years he has traveled the country as a keynote speaker – with a variety of invitations to camps, conferences, NASCAR, and the NFL. JC has one primary objective when invited to speak – enthusiastically share the message of hope and the love of Jesus Christ!

However, J.C.'s primary ministry is his family! He says, "There's a lot of dynamic speakers out there, but I'm the only one who can be a dad to my kids (Laiklan and London) and husband to my wife (Kimberly)!"

Alongside his wife, Kimberly, he pastors GO Church, a thriving multi-campus ministry with a heart to reach people everywhere.

JC is an Ordained Bishop in the Church of God (Cleveland, TN) and is a graduate of Lee University, where he obtained a Bachelor of Science degree in Pastoral Studies. He is currently pursuing his Master of Arts in Ministry Degree from Richmont Graduate University. He is the founder of GO U—a school of theology and ministry, and author of *Deeper21: Experience the Power of Prayer and Fasting in Twenty-One Days.* He is also the host of the popular On The GO podcast, where he shares insights on Life, Leadership, and the Lord.

For more information, or to enquire about speaking engagements email contact@deeper21.com.

ACKNOWLEDGMENTS

To my wife, Kimberly: this book belongs to you as much as it does to me. You reflect Jesus more clearly than anyone I know. Your grace, and unwavering love have been my anchor and my inspiration. Every page carries the imprint of your quiet strength and steadfast heart.

To my children, Laiklan and London: you are my pride and joy. Watching you grow reminds me that fatherhood is one of life's highest callings. It is an honor to be your dad. I pray that when you read these words one day, you'll see a legacy of love, faith, and obedience to God.

To my mother Dorothy, you've been through so much in your life, and you've never quit. I've watched you "keep on keepin on." You're strength and perseverance has been an example to me. I love you and am grateful that you're my mom.

To my GO Church family: thank you for the sacred privilege of being your pastor. It is the highest honor of my life to serve you and lead you closer to Christ. My prayer echoes Paul's words: "Follow my example, as I follow the example of Christ" (1 Corinthians 11:1).

And finally, to Richmont Graduate University: thank you for sharpening my mind, stirring my spirit, and stretching my capacity. This journey has refined both my theology and my soul.

NOTES

1. Fasting is mentioned about 77 times, and baptism is mentioned about 75 times. From Donald S. Whitney, *Spiritual Disciplines for the Christian Life* (The Navigators, 2014) 192.

2. Dalia Fahmy, "How Common Is Religious Fasting in the United States?" Pew Research Center, 5 Apr. 2024, www.pewresearch.org/short-reads/2024/04/05/how-common-is-religious-fasting-in-the-united-states/. Accessed 28 July, 2025.

3. Elmer L. Towns, *Fasting for Spiritual Breakthrough: A Practical Guide to Nine Biblical Fasts* (Baker Publishing Group, 2017), "The Fast God Chooses." Kindle Edition.

4. Augustine, Letter 130 to Proba, Nicene and Post-Nicene Fathers, Series I, Vol. 1, ed. Philip Schaff (Peabody, MA: Hendrickson, 1994), 433–438.

5. Kenneth J. Collins, *A Real Christian: The Life of John Wesley* (Abingdon Press, 1999), 31.

6. List adapted from Reward Sibanda, *How to Fast: Rediscover the Ancient Practice for Unlocking Physical, Emotional, and Spiritual Renewal* (PRH Christian Publishing, 2025), 7–9.

7. Charles Marsh, *Strange Glory: A Life of Dietrich Bonhoeffer,* (Knopf Doubleday Publishing Group, 2014), 232.

8. Dietrich Bonhoeffer, *The Cost of Discipleship*, trans. R. H. Fuller, rev. ed. (New York: The Macmillan Co., 1960), 54.

9. A comprehensive list includes solitude, silence, fasting, frugality, chastity, secrecy, sacrifice, study, worship, celebration, service, prayer, fellowship, confession, and submission. List from Dallas Willard, The *Spirit of the Disciplines* (HarperCollins, 1988), 156–191.

10. Tish Harrison Warren, *Liturgy of the Ordinary* (InterVarsity Press, 2016), 42.

11. Dallas Willard, *The Spirit of the Disciplines: Understanding How God Changes Lives* (HarperCollins, 1988), 152.

12. Eric Metaxas, *Martin Luther: The Man Who Rediscovered God and Changed the World* (Penguin Publishing Group, 2018), 32.

13. Eric Metaxas, *Martin Luther: The Man Who Rediscovered God and Changed the World* (Penguin Publishing Group, 2018), 46.

14. This is one of 4 reasons given by author John Mark Comer in his teaching on fasting. John Mark Comer (Host). (2021–present). John Mark Comer Teachings [Audio podcast]. Practicing the Way. https://podcasts.apple.com/us/podcast/offering-fasting-e1/id1592847144?i=1000664114594

15. Henri J. M. Nouwen, *The Way of the Heart: Connecting with God through Prayer, Wisdom, and Silence* (Ballantine Books, 1981), 9–10.

16. Henri J. M. Nouwen, *The Way of the Heart: Connecting with God through Prayer, Wisdom, and Silence* (Ballantine Books, 1981), 9–10.

17. E. G. Carre, Praying Hyde: *Apostle of Prayer, the Life Story of John Hyde* (Bridge-Logos Publishers, 1982), 11–12. Kindle Edition.

18. E. G. Carre, Praying Hyde: *Apostle of Prayer, the Life Story of John Hyde* (Bridge-Logos Publishers, 1982), 21–33. Kindle Edition.

19. Ignatius of Loyola, *The Autobiography of St. Ignatius* (Benziger Brothers, 1900, Public Domain) 3–4. Kindle Edition.

20. Jonathan Goforth, *By my Spirit* (SolidChristianBooks.com, 2015) 42.

21. Jonathan Goforth, *By my Spirit* (SolidChristianBooks.com, 2015) 13–14.

22. Richard J. Foster, *Celebration of Discipline, Special Anniversary Edition: The Path to Spiritual Growth* (HarperCollins, 2018), 55.

23. Dr. and Mrs. Howard Taylor, *Hudson Taylor's Spiritual Secret* (Benediction Classics, 2013), 22.

24. Mark Batterson, *The Circle Maker: Praying Circles Around Your Biggest Dreams and Greatest Fears* (Zondervan, 2011), 32.

25. Mark Batterson, *The Circle Maker: Praying Circles Around Your Biggest Dreams and Greatest Fears* (Zondervan, 2011), 32.

26. Eugene H. Peterson, *The Contemplative Pastor: Returning to the Art of*

Spiritual Direction (Wm. B. Eerdmans Publishing Co., 1993), 22.

27. Donald Sweeting and George *Sweeting, Lessons from the Life of Moody* (Chicago: Moody, 2001), 128–129.

28. Pete Greig, *How to Pray: A Simple Guide For Normal People* (NavPress, 2019) 30–31.

29. Pete Greig, *How to Pray: A Simple Guide For Normal People* (NavPress, 2019) 30–31.

30. C.S. Lewis, *Letters to Malcolm: Chiefly On Prayer.* (HarperOne, 2017), 156.

31. Jeremy Kinsley, *George Muller: A Life of Faith and Prayer* (Self-published, 2025), 92.

32. Norman P. Grubb, *Rees Howells: Intercessor* (CLC Publications, 1952), 171.

33. Norman P. Grubb, *Rees Howells: Intercessor* (CLC Publications, 1952), 171.

34. Dallas Willard, *The Divine Conspiracy: Rediscovering Our Hidden Life In God.* (HarperSanFrancisco, 1998), 243.

35. Eugene H. Peterson, *Answering God: The Psalms As Tools For Prayer* (HarperSanFrancisco, 1989), 3.

36. C. S. Lewis, *The Screwtape Letters* (HarperCollins, 1996), 17. (Original work published 1942)

37. Mark Batterson, *The Circle Maker: Praying Circles Around Your Biggest Dreams and Greatest Fears* (Zondervan, 2011) 109.

38. Mother Teresa; Brian Kolodiejchuk, *Mother Teresa: Come Be My Light: The Private Writings of the Saint of Calcutta* (PRH Christian Publishing, 2007), 39–40.

39. Mother Teresa, *In the Heart of the World: Thoughts, Stories, and Prayers* (New World Library, 1997), 19.

40. Pete Greig, *How To Hear God: A Simple Guide For Normal People* (Zondervan, 2022), 19.

41. Jonathan Edwards, *The Life and Diary of David Brainerd* (Moody Publishers, 1980), Part 1. Kindle Edition.

42. "Catching the Missionary Spirit." The Master's Seminary, 31 Jan. 2024, https://blog.tms.edu/catching-the-missionary-spirit. Accessed 15 August, 2025.

43. Sam Wellman, *William Carey* (Wild Centuries Press, 2013), 29.

44. Tom Ascol, "A Lingering Obligation." Ligonier Ministries, 26 Dec. 2008, learn.ligonier.org/devotionals/lingering-obligation. Accessed 11 Aug. 2025.

45. David Wilkerson, *The Cross and the Switchblade* (Grand Rapids: Revell, 1963), 28–34.

46. Brother Andrew, *God's Smuggler* (Baker Publishing Group, 2015), 107–108.

47. David Smithers, "The 1949 Hebrides Intercessors." The Revival Library, https://revival-library.org/david-smithers/1949-hebrides-intercessors/. Accessed 15 August, 2025.

48. Duncan Campbell, *The Lewis Awakening* (Kraus House, 2015) , "How it began," Kindle Edition.

49. Kenneth J. Collins, *A Real Christian: The Life of John Wesley* (Abingdon Press, 1999), 31.

50. "The Wesley Fast." Methodist Prayer, https://methodistprayer.org/wesleyfast. Accessed 15 August, 2025.

51. A. W. Tozer, *The Pursuit of God: The Human Thirst for the Divine* (Moody Publishers, 2007) "The Universal Presence," Kindle Edition.

52. Charles G. Finney, *The Autobiography of Charles G. Finney: The Life Story of America's Greatest Evangelist—In His Own Words* (Baker Publishing Group, 2012), 94.

53. Steve Porter, Daniel Nash: *Laborer with Finney. Mighty in Prayer* (Christian History and Revival Book 1) (Deeper Life Press, 2021), 16–17.

Made in the USA
Middletown, DE
22 January 2026